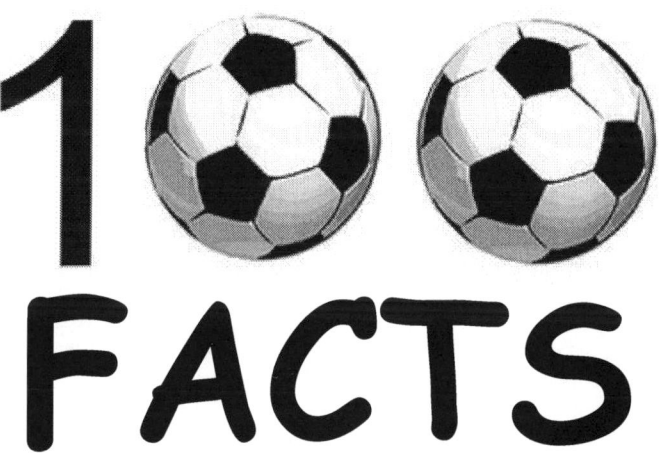

FACTS

SUNDERLAND

FACTS

SUNDERLAND

Steve Horton

Bedford, England

First published in Great Britain in 2021
by Wymer Publishing
www.wymerpublishing.co.uk
Wymer Publishing is a trading name of Wymer (UK) Ltd

First edition. Copyright © 2021 Steve Horton / Wymer Publishing.

ISBN 978-1-912782-80-2

Edited by Jerry Bloom.

The Author hereby asserts his rights to be identified
as the author of this work in accordance with sections
77 to 78 of the Copyright, Designs & Patents Act 1988.

All rights reserved. No part of this publication may be
reproduced or transmitted in any form or by any means,
electronic or mechanical, including photocopying, or any
information storage and retrieval system, without written
permission from the publisher.

This publication is sold subject to the condition that it shall not,
by way of trade or otherwise, be lent, re-sold, hired out or
otherwise circulated without the publishers prior consent in any
form of binding or cover other than that in which it is published
and without a similar condition including this condition
being imposed on the subsequent purchaser.

Typeset and Design by Andy Bishop / 1016 Sarpsborg
Printed by CMP, Poole, Dorset

A catalogue record for this book is available from the British Library.

Sketches © Becky Welton-Fodder & Amy McIsaac.

1879/1880
SUNDERLAND & DISTRICT TEACHERS FC

FACT 1

There is no firm evidence as to the exact foundation date of Sunderland Association Football Club. For over a century it was recorded as 1879, but in the 21st Century research has indicated 1880 was more likely.

What is certain, verifiable by newspaper reports, is that club founder James Allan was appointed as an assistant master at Hendon Board School in April 1879.

At that time, only rugby football was played in the town and Allan introduced the association code to his colleagues. They were all members of the Sunderland & District Teachers Association.

In September 1880 the *Sunderland Daily Echo* reported that the teachers' association had formed a football club at a meeting in Rectory Park. They then rented the Blue House Field but it was soon apparent that there would not be enough teachers to raise a team. This led to membership being open to all and a name change to Sunderland AFC.

The first recorded game took place against Ferryhill at Blue House Field on 15th November 1880 and ended in a 1-0 defeat. That season the club also entered the newly created Northumberland & Durham Challenge Cup.

Opinions continue to differ on the date of foundation. Allan and other founding members may well have been playing football together in 1879, but it does seem that an actual club was not formed until 1880.

1884
DURHAM CHALLENGE CUP WINNERS

FACT 2

Sunderland won their first trophy in 1884. They beat Darlington in the replayed final of the Durham Challenge Cup, the first game having been declared void following a protest by the opposition.

This was the first season of the competition and Sunderland had comfortable home wins over Milkwell Burn, Jarrow and Hamsterley Rangers to reach the semi-finals. They drew 0-0 with Hobson Wanderers before thrashing them 6-0 in the replay.

The final against Darlington was played at Newcastle Road. This was not yet Sunderland's home ground, but still a venue where they enjoyed the majority of the support and they won an exciting game 4-3. However, a Darlington appeal, stating that their own players and umpires were subject to threats of violence by spectators, was upheld.

The Durham FA ordered the final to be replayed at the neutral venue of Birtley. Early in the second half S. Joyce (his first name has been lost to history) opened the scoring for Sunderland. Jock McDonald added another by rushing the Darlington goalkeeper over the line while he had the ball, which was within the rules at the time.

Sunderland held out for a 2-0 victory and this time there were no opposition protests. However, the competition organisers had somehow forgotten to source a trophy and it was not presented to Sunderland until the following January.

FACT 3
1884
ABBS FIELD

Sunderland moved to their fifth ground in just five years of existence in 1884. However, the significance of Abbs Field in Fulwell was that they were able to charge spectators for entry.

The first four grounds were all on open fields. Admission fees couldn't be charged but as interest grew, the club looked for somewhere that they could control entrance to the playing area.

Sunderland's first game at Abbs Field was a friendly against Birtley on 27th September. Goals from Jock McDonald and John Grayston gave Sunderland a 2-1 victory.

Playing at Abbs Field allowed Sunderland to enter the FA Cup for the first time, although they never got to play a home tie at the ground. Another significant development is that they started playing in red and white stripes whilst there. They also enjoyed a 23-0 victory over Castletown in a friendly.

Sunderland enjoyed a great record at Abbs Field, losing just three games there. One of these was an 11-1 thrashing by Scottish touring side Port Glasgow Athletic.

After two years at Abbs Field Sunderland were on the move again due to a rent increase. The site of the ground is now covered by housing.

FACT 4
1884
ENTERING
THE FA CUP

Sunderland entered the FA Cup for the first time in the 1884-85 season. However, their participation was short lived as they were beaten 3-1 by Redcar in the first round.

Redcar were drawn at home and the attendance was described as large despite the cold and windy weather on a November afternoon. In the first half Sunderland were against the wind and conceded three times. The second goal, scored by Redcar's captain W. Harrison, was an overhead kick which was 'loudly applauded' according to the *York Herald*.

In the second half, with the wind in their favour, Sunderland did far better. They pulled a goal back almost immediately but another effort soon afterwards was ruled out for offside. Despite enjoying plenty of possession, they were unable to get back into the game and it finished 3-1.

In the next round Redcar were knocked out by Grimsby Town. Sunderland fared better in that season's Durham Challenge Cup. They reached the final but failed to retain the trophy, being beaten 3-0 by Darlington.

In the following season's FA Cup Sunderland were drawn away to Redcar again in the first round. They again failed to progress, this time losing 3-0.

FACT 5
1886
NEWCASTLE ROAD

After two seasons at Abbs Field, Sunderland were on the move again in 1886. They became tenants at Newcastle Road, where they were able to increase capacity by building stands.

The decision to leave Abbs Field was an easy one due to the landlord demanding a fivefold rent increase. They agreed a deal to rent Newcastle Road in Monkwearmouth from the Thompson sisters, who owned a local shipyard.

Labourers from the shipyard were used for building work and the ground had a capacity of around 15,000. Sunderland's first game there as the home team was on 10th April when they drew 3-3 in a friendly with Birtley.

On 30th October, Newcastle Road hosted Sunderland's first home game in the FA Cup, a 2-1 victory over Newcastle West End. It was also Sunderland's home when they joined the Football League in 1890. Although the official capacity was 15,000, a crowd of 21,000 did squeeze in for an FA Cup tie against Everton in 1891. At the time it was a record crowd for a football match in England.

Sunderland remained at Newcastle Road for twelve years, during which time they won three league championships. It was only the ground's limitations for future expansion that led them to leave.

FACT 6
1887
DISQUALIFIED
FROM THE FA CUP

Sunderland thought they had beaten Middlesbrough in a keenly contested FA Cup tie in December 1887. However, they were subsequently disqualified from the competition for fielding ineligible players.

Two special trains took 3,000 Sunderland supporters to Middlesbrough for this tie on 26th November. They were delighted to see their team lead 2-0 at half time, but when play restarted they were up against a strong wind and the home side scored twice to force a replay.

The following weekend at Newcastle Road, travelling fans made up about a third of the 9,000 crowd. Sunderland trailed 2-0 at half time but in a sensational start to the second half, scored three times in seven minutes. As Middlesbrough chased an equaliser, Tam Halliday scored a fourth with three minutes remaining.

Three weeks later at a hearing in Darlington, Sunderland were thrown out of the competition. The rules at the time stated that professionals could only play in the FA Cup if they had lived within six miles of the club's ground for at least two years. As three of Sunderland's players had only arrived from Scotland in August, it meant they had been ineligible.

In the following round Middlesbrough beat London side Old Foresters before losing to Crewe Alexandra in the quarter final.

FACT 7
1888
SUNDERLAND ALBION

In March 1888 Sunderland's founder James Allan, unhappy at the direction the club was taking, left to form Sunderland Albion. However, they were in existence for just four years.

Allan did not like the increasing commercialism at Sunderland and on leaving, seven players decided to join him at the new club. Sunderland and Albion soon became fierce rivals, and when they were drawn to face each other in the FA Cup the following season, Sunderland withdrew. This was because they did not want to see Albion benefit from a share of the gate receipts.

Due to increasing demand amongst the public, Sunderland did agree to host two friendly matches against Albion. The first of these in December 1888 attracted a huge crowd of 15,000, with Sunderland winning 2-0. The second in January also ended in a Sunderland victory, 3-2. Gate receipts from the 9,000 crowd at the second match were given to charity.

In 1889 Sunderland Albion joined the Football Alliance, which was seen as the strongest competition outside the Football League. However, when Sunderland gained election to the Football League in 1890, it was a bitter blow to Albion. In 1891 they withdrew from the Alliance due to the cost of travelling and the following year folded completely.

FACT 8
1890
THE TEAM
OF ALL THE TALENTS

Sunderland's expensively assembled squad was dubbed 'The Team Of All The Talents' in 1890. This phrase was coined to reflect them having a top-quality player in each position.

Sunderland were not one of the twelve founder members of the Football League in 1888. However, they played a number of friendlies against those clubs and more than held their own. In 1889-90 they played eleven games against Football League opposition at Newcastle Road, winning six and losing just two.

The most astonishing result was a 7-2 victory over Aston Villa on 5th April. Villa board member William McGregor, whose idea it was to found the Football League, said afterwards that Sunderland had "a talented man in every position". The *Sunderland Daily Echo* saw the remarks as sarcastic at first, but soon began to adopt the phrase themselves.

Under the leadership of Tom Watson, the 'Team of All The Talents' won three league titles between 1892 and 1895. They also beat Hearts in Edinburgh to be declared world champions. However, the FA Cup, for which the squad was first assembled prior to Football League membership, was to elude them.

FACT 9
1890
ELECTION TO THE
FOOTBALL LEAGUE

When Sunderland were elected to the Football League in 1890, they became the first new club to join it since its formation two years earlier.

Sunderland were elected in place of Stoke City, who had finished bottom in both of the Football League's two seasons so far. They had good playing credentials, having impressed against league sides in friendlies. Their remote location was a worry so they offered to pay the travelling expenses of teams to the North East to ensure the vote went their way.

In the first half of the season Sunderland struggled. They lost their first two games and a 2-1 defeat at Notts County on 15th December left them bottom of the table. However, a 1-0 win over eventual champions Everton in their next game was the catalyst for an upturn in form. They lost just one of their last ten games, winning six in a row at home.

Sunderland eventually finished sixth from twelve teams, with eleven wins, two draws and nine defeats. Johnny Campbell was leading scorer with eighteen goals and the average attendance at Newcastle Road was 6,818.

FACT 10
1892
CHAMPIONS FOR THE FIRST TIME

In just their second season in the Football League, Sunderland were champions. They won all thirteen home games and scored an incredible 93 goals in 26 matches.

Sunderland beat Wolverhampton Wanderers 5-2 at home in their first game but then lost the next three, all away. This meant they were bottom of the table at the end of September but they went on to lose just two of the remaining 22 games. The other twenty were all won with not a single game being drawn all season.

At home Sunderland were invincible. They scored at least two goals in every game and hit four or more on ten occasions at Newcastle Road. They scored plenty on their travels too, hitting seven at Darwen and five at Accrington and West Bromwich Albion. Forward Jimmy Campbell was the Football League's leading scorer, with 31 goals in 24 appearances.

The title was secured in style in Sunderland's last home game, against Blackburn Rovers. They thrashed the visitors 6-1, with Campbell scoring four. They then won their last two away games to finish on 42 points, five clear of runners up Preston North End.

FACT 11
1893
RETAINING
THE TITLE IN STYLE

Sunderland won the Football League Championship for the second season running in 1892-93. They enjoyed an even bigger winning margin than a year earlier and scored 100 goals.

The Football League was expanded, with two teams added as well as the formation of a Second Division. Sunderland began the season in devastating fashion with a 6-0 win at Accrington and then won 6-1 away to Aston Villa in their third game.

For most of the first half of the season Sunderland were in second place behind Preston North End. However, in January they won five matches in a row to seize the title initiative. These included a 2-1 win at Preston followed by a 6-0 home thrashing of third placed Villa.

Sunderland lost just once after New Year, at Bolton on 1st April. On the same day, Preston surprisingly lost to bottom club Newton Heath. This meant they could only be denied the title if they lost their last three games by a massive margin. They made no mistake in their next game, hammering Newton Heath 6-0 at Newcastle Road.

In their final two games Sunderland drew 1-1 at Derby County and won 3-2 at Burnley. This meant they finished the season 11 points clear of Preston and with 100 goals. Johnny Campbell was again the league's leading scorer, this time with thirty goals.

FACT 12
1894
A GAME OF
THREE HALVES

On the opening day of the 1894-95 season, Sunderland beat Derby County 8-0 at Newcastle Road. It remains the club's best ever home league victory and was known as the 'game of three halves' due to it being abandoned and starting again.

The game started with a replacement referee, John Conqueror, as the designated official Thomas Kirkham was running late. By the time Kirkham arrived it was half time and Sunderland were leading 3-0.

Conqueror had lived locally and Kirkham sensationally annulled the first 45 minutes to play a whole ninety with him in charge. Not surprisingly Derby made no protests about this.

A supposedly more 'neutral' referee still did nothing to help Derby. Jimmy Hannah scored after just four minutes and Sunderland again led 3-0 at half time. In the second half, they scored five more to record an 8-0 score line. Jimmy Millar, Tommy Hyslop and Johnny Campbell each scored two goals, with the other coming from James Gillespie.

A jaded Derby had effectively been beaten 11-0 over two hours and fifteen minutes. Sunderland finished the season as champions. In contrast, Derby were relieved to avoid relegation via the test matches.

FACT 13

1895
A CORNER KICK

The oldest painting in the world depicting a football match hangs in the lobby at the Stadium of Light. Thomas Hemy's *A Corner Kick* features a game between Sunderland and Aston Villa that took place at Newcastle Road on 2nd January 1895.

Sunderland and Villa were great rivals and during the 1890s won seven titles between them. When they faced each other at Newcastle Road, Sunderland were top of the league but led reigning champions Villa by just one point.

In a thrilling game, Sunderland came from 3-1 down to lead 4-3, only for Villa to equalise with ten minutes remaining. Sunderland eventually went on to win the title, with Villa finishing in third behind Everton.

Hemy was at the match but painted it from memory. At the bottom of the painting are players' names and it is interesting to see straw at the side of the pitch. This was commonly used then to protect it from frost. Sunderland purchased the painting from Hemy in 1898.

In the 1920s the painting was displayed in a pub belonging to the chairman's family. It was given back to the club in 1930 and remained at Roker Park until 1990. It was then loaned to the Sunderland Museum & Art Gallery before being displayed at the Stadium of Light when it opened in 1997.

FACT 14
1895
CHAMPIONS OF
THE WORLD

Sunderland were Football League champions for the third time in 1894-95. They then beat Scottish side Heart of Midlothian in a match dubbed as the Football World Championship.

Sunderland topped the table from January but didn't clinch the title until their last game of the season. On 20th April they beat Everton 2-1 in front of 20,000 spectators at Newcastle Road to secure a third title in five years. Just a week later they were taking part in a match to decide who could be dubbed world champions.

On the morning of 27th April Sunderland's players and officials took the train to Edinburgh, had lunch in a hotel then a stroll in the city prior to the 4pm kick off. Hearts had the better of the early stages but Ned Doig in the Sunderland goal was on top form to deny them.

Sunderland grew into the game and led 2-0 at half time, only for Hearts to hit back and lead 3-2. Johnny Campbell scored twice to put Sunderland back in front but Hearts fought hard for an equaliser. With two minutes to go John Harvey scored a breakaway goal, running solo from the halfway line to complete a stunning 5-3 win for Sunderland.

Sunderland held the title of 'world champions' for five years as the next time such a contest took place was 1901.

FACT 15
1896
TOM WATSON
GOES TO LIVERPOOL

Sunderland manager Tom Watson caused a football sensation in 1896. He left the team that he had led to three league titles to become manager at Liverpool, who had just been promoted to the First Division.

Watson was just thirty years old when he came to Sunderland in 1889. He had already been a successful general manager with Newcastle West End and Newcastle East End. At Sunderland he was given control over selecting the team, which up until then had been done by a committee.

Many of Watson's recruits were from Scotland and his team were champions in 1892, only their second season in the Football League. They retained the title the following season and won it again in 1895. In between, they had finished second in 1894.

In 1896 Liverpool, who had only been in existence for four years, were promoted straight back to the First Division after being relegated in the season that Sunderland won their third title. Determined not to be a yo-yo club, their directors offered Watson double his Sunderland salary to entice him to Merseyside.

Sunderland struggled in their first season without Watson and were nearly relegated. Their former manager had more success at Liverpool, winning the title in 1901 and 1906. He is buried in Anfield Cemetery where his headstone contains the Sunderland crest.

FACT 16

1897
TEST MATCHES SAVE SUNDERLAND

Just two years after they finished as champions of the Football League, Sunderland faced relegation in 1897. They managed to stay up thanks to their results in a series of test matches.

Sunderland won just seven of their thirty games and finished in fifteenth place. There was no automatic promotion and relegation, with the bottom two sides in the First Division facing the top two in the Second to determine who played where the following season.

Sunderland's first test match was away to Notts County, who had finished top of the Second Division. The first game in Nottingham on 17th April was a 1-0 defeat then two days later the two sides drew 0-0 at Newcastle Road.

Newton Heath (later Manchester United) were Sunderland's next opponents. After a 1-1 draw at Bank Street Manchester, Sunderland won their home game 2-0. Teams from the same division did not play each other in test matches. This meant that Sunderland had no games against Burnley, who had finished bottom of the First Division.

The final table after four games placed Sunderland in second place. Even then this did not guarantee survival, it had to be ratified by Football League members. However, Sunderland's standing in the game meant they had little difficulty in securing enough votes to get re-elected back to the First Division.

FACT 17
1898
ROKER PARK

In 1898 Sunderland said farewell to Newcastle Road and moved to a purpose-built home at Roker Park, where they would remain for 99 years.

Sunderland's success on the field led to a rise in attendances, but Newcastle Road held only 15,000 and expansion opportunities were limited. The club became a limited company with the money raised from selling shares used to fund the purchase of farmland to build a new ground.

It took just three months to build the wooden grandstand with paddock in front and a covered standing area opposite. On 10th September the ground was officially opened by the Marquess of Londonderry for Sunderland's First Division fixture against Liverpool. In his speech, the Marquess said that football was a game of determination and indomitable courage, qualities which were great characteristics of Englishmen.

The game was watched by a crowd of 30,000 and well contested, with Liverpool being the better side early on but Sunderland gaining in confidence as it progressed. There were no goals at half time and after having the better of the second half, Jim Leslie scored six minutes from time to give Sunderland a 1-0 victory.

FACT 18

1901
THE GOOD
FRIDAY RIOT

The Tyne-Wear derby at St James Park on Good Friday was abandoned before kick off in chaotic circumstances. There were more than twice as many in the ground than its official capacity, and rioting broke out when the game was called off.

There was huge interest in the game, as Sunderland were top of the table and Newcastle seventh. It was a fine day and it was soon clear that there were far more fans present than the 30,000 the ground was supposed to hold.

At 3pm the gates were locked with 20,000 still outside. Newspapers reported that the gates were then broken down and people clambered like cats over walls. With the terraces packed, fans spilled onto the pitch and the police were unable to clear it. There were also hundreds perched dangerously on the roof of the stand, a section of which gave way causing panic in the seating below.

At 3:30pm the teams pushed their way onto the field, hoping this would force crowds to disperse. The referee decided play was impossible and abandoned the game. There was then riotous behaviour that saw the goalposts ripped out, flags torn down and bottles thrown.

When the game was eventually replayed three weeks later, Sunderland won 2-0. They eventually finished second in the table.

FACT 19

1904
THE McCOMBIE AFFAIR

Sunderland were rocked during the 1903-04 season when they were found guilty of financial irregularities. It led to the club being handed a large fine and several directors being suspended.

During the season right back Andy McCombie was loaned £100 by the club to start a business. This was on the basis he would repay it from the receipts of a benefit game. When this took place, he refused to do so, believing the money was a bonus.

The club took McCombie to court and a judgement ruled in their favour. However, when the Football Association intervened, they took the side of McCombie. A further audit of the club's accounts found a number of irregular payments.

Six club directors were suspended for two and a half years and a fine of £250 was imposed. Manager Alex McKie was given a short suspension but resigned anyway, taking over at Middlesbrough. The following year he became embroiled in a payments scandal there and left the game altogether.

McCombie was transferred to Newcastle where he enjoyed six successful years as a player and then forty more on their coaching staff.

FACT 20
1904
NED DOIG LEAVES

In 1904 goalkeeper Ned Doig left Sunderland after fourteen years at the club. During that time he had been a virtual ever present in goal and made over 450 appearances.

Doig was already a Scottish international when Sunderland signed him in 1890, taking advantage of a disagreement he had with Blackburn Rovers. He was only five feet nine inches tall but made up for that with his athleticism and refusal to give up.

In fourteen seasons with Sunderland, Doig won four league titles and made 417 First Division appearances, as well as forty more in other competitions.

By the summer of 1904 Doig was 37 years old and when the board offered him reduced terms, he refused to sign a new contract even when they agreed to meet his demands. Doig then agreed to join former manager Tom Watson at Liverpool, even though they had just been relegated to the Second Division.

Doig remained at Liverpool for four seasons and is their oldest ever player. He died in 1919 and lay in an unmarked grave for decades. The plot is now marked by a stone bearing the crests of both Sunderland and Liverpool.

FACT 21
1905
ALF COMMON'S FOUR-FIGURE TRANSFER

Sunderland were involved in a transfer sensation in February 1905. Their inside forward Alf Common was sold to struggling Middlesbrough for a new record fee of £1,000.

In October 1901 Common had been sold by Sunderland to Sheffield United. He was an instant success, scoring in their FA Cup final win that season. By 1904 he was an England international and wanted to return to the North East, with Sunderland agreeing to pay £520 to bring him back to Roker Park.

Common scored six goals in 22 appearances for Sunderland that season. The last of these was in a 1-1 home draw with Wolves in the FA Cup on 4th February. The replay, which Sunderland lost 1-0 turned out to be his last game for the club.

On 14th February Sunderland agreed to allow Common to be transferred to Middlesbrough for £1,000. It was the first time a British club had paid a four-figure sum for a player. What was most surprising was that Middlesbrough were battling relegation and looked to be trying to buy their way out of trouble. For Sunderland, it was too big a fee to refuse.

Common's first game for Middlesbrough was a friendly against Sunderland four days after the transfer. The Rokerites came from a goal down to win 2-1.

FACT 22

1908
NEWCASTLE 1
SUNDERLAND 9

Sunderland's record league victory was on 5th December 1908 and came in the Tyne-Wear derby. They thrashed Newcastle 9-1, with eight of their goals coming in the second half.

Billy Hogg opened the scoring after seven minutes with a simple tap in. Play was even for the remainder of the half and Newcastle equalised two minutes before the break from the penalty spot after a handball by Charlie Thomson.

Early in the second half Sunderland regained the lead with a fine drive by George Holley. Soon after Hogg scored his second and Newcastle's half and fullbacks simply capitulated in the face of Sunderland's swift play.

It was too easy for Sunderland's wingers to get the ball up field and either shoot for goal themselves or set up the forwards. Holley scored the fourth and fifth goals to complete his hat trick. Arthur Bridgett got the sixth and seventh then Jackie Mordue, who had set up Hogg's goals, scored one for himself.

Hogg finished the scoring but neither hat-trick scorer claimed the match ball. It was instead taken by Sunderland's keeper Leigh Roose, who potentially had only seen it when picking it out of the net from the penalty.

Bizarrely, Newcastle went on to become champions that season. The result remained the biggest away win in topflight history until 2019 when Leicester won 9-0 at Southampton.

FACT 23
1911
FIRST RECORD DEFEAT

Sunderland's record defeat is 8-0, a score line they have been on the wrong end of on four occasions. The first of these was on Boxing Day 1911, when it was inflicted upon them by Sheffield Wednesday.

Wednesday took the lead after just four minutes but didn't get their second until shortly after Sunderland skipper Charlie Thomson went off injured midway through the half. Sunderland then completely fell apart without their captain and were 7-0 down at half time as Wednesday took advantage of the lack of commanding presence in the centre of defence.

For the second half Thomson did manage to take the field but was virtually a passenger. Sunderland however, were far better organised and the home crowd sportingly cheered any clearances and saves.

With ten minutes remaining Wednesday, who had been playing at a much slower pace, scored an eighth goal. Sunderland suffered a further blow when keeper Walter Scott collided with a post and had to be taken to hospital with concussion.

Sunderland's previous record defeat had been 8-1 at Blackburn Rovers. They have since lost 8-0 at West Ham United (1968), Watford (1982) and Southampton (2014).

FACT 24

1913
RECORD CROWD
FOR FA CUP FINAL

Sunderland went close to doing the Double of Football League Championship and FA Cup in 1912-13. However, they were beaten 1-0 in the cup final by Aston Villa in front of a record crowd of over 120,000 at Crystal Palace.

Sunderland's run to the final included victory over Newcastle in a quarter final tie that needed two replays. After a 0-0 draw at Roker Park, the two sides drew 2-2 at St James' Park which was also the venue for the second replay, which Sunderland won 3-0. They then beat Burnley 3-2 in a semi-final replay at St Andrews, Birmingham, after the first game had ended 0-0 at Bramall Lane, Sheffield.

This was the first time the showpiece game had been contested by the top two sides in the league and the attendance was recorded as 121,919. This was a world record and has been bettered only once in England, for the 1923 final.

Nerves got the better of Sunderland and they failed to play to their usual standards. There were several disruptions due to fouling caused by a long-standing feud involving Sunderland's Charlie Thomson and Villa's Harry Hampton. The game was settled by Thomas Barber's goal twelve minutes from full time. Sunderland had to wait 24 more years to get their hands on the trophy.

FACT 25
1913
AN UNLIKELY TITLE TRIUMPH

A week after losing the FA Cup final to Aston Villa, Sunderland pipped them to the Football League Championship. Their triumph had seemed an unlikely one earlier in the season after they failed to win any of their first seven games.

Sunderland were in the relegation zone at the beginning of October, after a 2-0 defeat at Chelsea made it seven games without a win from the start of the season.

However, the arrival of new goalkeeper Joe Butler and full back Charlie Gladwin strengthened the defence and results soon started to improve. Five straight wins lifted Sunderland out of danger and by New Year they were up to fifth, going top in February.

After losing the cup final on 12th April, Sunderland travelled to Villa Park for a top of the table clash four days later. Walter Tinsley scored in a 1-1 draw that kept Sunderland in the driving seat for the title.

In their penultimate game, away to Bolton Wanderers, Sunderland won 3-1 to clinch the title with a game to spare. They then rounded off the season with a 1-0 win over Bradford City in front of 15,000 fans at Roker Park. This took their point total to 54, a record at the time and an inconceivable concept back in the autumn.

FACT 26
1922
WORLD RECORD FEE
FOR WARNEY CRESSWELL

Sunderland broke the world transfer record in 1922 when they paid £5,500 for full back Warney Cresswell.

Creswell was 24 years old when he joined the Black Cats from South Shields, who were then in the Second Division, in March 1922. His was the highest profile of three new signings in 24 hours, the others being Joc Paterson and Mike Gilhooley.

An England international right back, Cresswell had developed a reputation as a firm tackler who won the ball cleanly. He had a cool head and a good sense of positional play, with the ability to bring the ball forward rather than just launch it up field.

Cresswell was appointed Sunderland's captain during the 1923-24 season. They looked set to win the league, only to suffer a late collapse by losing their last two matches and eventually finished third. In total he made 182 appearances for the Black Cats, but never scored a goal.

During Cresswell's five full seasons with Sunderland, the club finished second once and third on three occasions. He was sold to Everton in 1927 where he won the title in his first season and in the late 1930s he managed Port Vale and Northampton Town. After quitting football he returned to Sunderland and ran the Sheet Anchor pub in Dundas Street.

FACT 27

1925
SUNDERLAND'S RECORD
LEAGUE GOALSCORER

Sunderland's record goalscorer in league games is Charlie Buchan. By the time he left the club in 1925, he had scored 209 goals in 379 appearances.

Buchan was spotted by scouts playing in the Southern League for Leyton and joined the Black Cats as a nineteen-year-old in 1911. He was a tall all-round sportsman who also had a brief spell playing cricket for Durham in the Minor Counties Championship.

The First World War interrupted Buchan's football career, but he was just as prolific on either side of it. He was the Black Cats' top scorer seven times, including the 1912-13 title winning season. He captained the club in the 1920s and was hugely influential to those around him. He was also capped by England on six occasions.

In 1925 Arsenal, where Buchan had played as an amateur, agreed a deal for him to return to London. It was a sensational transfer story as despite being almost 34 years old, Buchan was still seen as one of the greatest players of the day.

Buchan spent three seasons with Arsenal, averaging a goal every other game. In later life Buchan was a journalist and edited a monthly magazine, *Charles Buchan's Football Monthly*.

FACT 28
1928
BOB KYLE LEAVES

In 1928 Bob Kyle, Sunderland's longest serving manager, left the club. He had been in charge for 23 years.

Kyle was 35 years old when he was appointed ahead of around seventy other applicants following Alex Mackie's departure to Middlesbrough. He had impressed with Distillery in the Irish League, winning three titles as well as two Irish Cups.

The first three seasons under Kyle's management were unspectacular. He was slowly dismantling the side he inherited and putting his own together, with Charlie Buchan's arrival in 1911 being the final piece of the jigsaw. This all paid off in 1912-13 when Sunderland won their fifth league title and reached the FA Cup final.

When the Football League resumed following the First World War, the Black Cats regularly challenged for the title, but kept falling short. They finished second to Liverpool in 1923 then in 1924 looked set to be champions only to blow it by losing their last two games.

Kyle's departure in 1928 came after a forgettable season in which Sunderland were almost relegated for the first time in their history. On the final day they beat Middlesbrough 3-0 at Roker Park, condemning their North East rivals to the drop instead. After 23 years and 817 games in charge the board decided it was now time for change.

1929
DAVE HALLIDAY
LEAVES

Dave Halliday, whose goals per game ratio at Sunderland was almost one per game, left the club in 1929. In four seasons at the club he had scored 165 goals in 175 games, including twelve hat tricks.

Halliday was signed from Dundee in 1925 and had a hard act to follow, having been bought to replace Charlie Buchan. He became an instant success, scoring 42 goals in his first season, 38 of them in the league.

In four seasons with Sunderland, Halliday was leading scorer in all of them, with a minimum of 35 goals each time. No other player has ever been able to match his worst season for the Black Cats. He took just 101 games to reach 100 league goals, the fastest striker in the English game to do so.

Halliday scored twelve hat tricks for the Black Cats, more than any other player. Three of these were four goal hauls. His 165 goals puts him third in the chart of all-time leading scorers for the club.

In 1928-29 Halliday's 43 goals made him the leading scorer in the Football League. He was signed by ambitious Arsenal but couldn't force his way into the team and soon moved on to Manchester City after just fifteen appearances in a year.

FACT 30
1933
RECORD CROWD

Sunderland's record attendance for a home fixture was set at an FA Cup quarter final replay on 8th March 1933. A massive 75,118 crammed into Roker Park to see them lose 1-0 to Derby County.

There was huge interest in the game and many factories closed for the afternoon. A dozen special trains were laid on from Newcastle and the town saw traffic jams like never before. The gates were locked an hour before kick off with 30,000 still outside.

Inside, ambulance crews had to revive hundreds of fans who fainted due to the crush, while many had to be moved onto the cinder track surrounding the pitch. Thousands more suffered from aching limbs and ribs.

In the game itself the Black Cats had a strike from Bobby Gurney ruled out for offside midway through the first half. An injury to Gurney then forced him onto the wing, causing serious disruption to the home side's attack. The only goal of the game was for Derby in extra time and Sunderland's dream of reaching the final was over.

The official attendance of 75,118 was 12,000 more than the ground's previous record. It was also a new record for a midweek match anywhere in England. By the time Sunderland left Roker Park in 1997, its capacity was down to just 22,500.

FACT 31
1935
SUNDERLAND'S OLDEST PLAYER

On 22nd April 1935 Tommy Urwin set the record for Sunderland's oldest player, which still stands today. He was 39 years and 76 days old when he appeared at outside left in an away game against Preston North End,

Urwin, who was mainly an outside right but could play on either flank, was 34 years old when he joined Sunderland from Newcastle in 1930. An England international with four caps, he is one of the few players to appear for all three North East clubs, having started his career with Middlesbrough.

Over the 1930-31 and 1931-32 seasons Urwin made 54 appearances, some of them as an emergency centre forward. He was known for his battling qualities and refusal to give up. Urwin's services were retained in 1932 but mainly as a player-coach, so he could help others develop in the reserves.

Over the busy Easter schedule in 1934-35, Jimmy Connor picked up an injury on the Saturday at Birmingham City. This led to the emergency inclusion of Urwin in the Black Cats' side for the game at Preston on Easter Monday. Reports state that he played reasonably well and could even have scored at one point but chose to pass instead. For the second half he dropped back into midfield and the game finished 1-1.

FACT 32

1936
THE LAST CHAMPIONSHIP

Sunderland won the Football League Championship for the sixth and last time in 1935-36.

After finishing runners up in 1934-35, Sunderland opened the new season with a trip to champions Arsenal. They lost 3-1 at Highbury but soon found form and won five out of their next six.

The Black Cats led the table from the middle of November and their forwards were in devastating form. They hit 109 goals, with five or more goals scored in a game on eight occasions. Raich Carter and Bobby Gurney both found the net 31 times, although five of Carter's goals were penalties.

The title was secured in style on 13th April, when the Black Cats thrashed Birmingham City 7-2 at St Andrews. A large contingent made their way from Wearside, travelling through the night. Some of these were invited to party with the players at their hotel, where a telegram of congratulations awaited from the deposed champions Arsenal.

There were still three games remaining and Sunderland lost two of these. Despite this, they finished comfortably top of the table with 56 points, eight points ahead of second place Derby County. Sunderland couldn't build on this and finished eighth the following season and have not been champions since.

FACT 33
1936
THE DEATH OF JIMMY THORPE

Sunderland's title triumph in 1936 was tinged with sadness. Goalkeeper Jimmy Thorpe died after being kicked in the chest in a match against Chelsea, leading to a change in the laws of the game.

The fatal game took place at Roker Park on 1st February. Thorpe conceded two goals in a minute as the visitors came from 3-1 down to draw 3-3. Press reports described both goals as keeper errors. Earlier in the game, he had been kicked in the head whilst lying on the ground with the ball, something which almost certainly affected his ability.

After the game Thorpe was taken ill at home and he died four days later in hospital. An inquest concluded that the cause of death was diabetes and heart failure, accelerated by rough usage of the opposing team. Thorpe, who had joined Sunderland from school, was just 22 years old and left a widow and three-year-old son.

Thorpe's death led to a change in the rules prohibiting players from kicking a ball that was in the keeper's hands. When Sunderland met Chelsea in 2011 on the 75th anniversary of his death, the keepers from both sides wore black armbands in his memory.

FACT 34
1936 CHARITY SHIELD WINNERS

Sunderland's only success in the Charity Shield (now Community Shield) was in 1936. The Football League Champions faced FA Cup winners Arsenal at Roker Park and won 2-1 thanks to a controversial late goal by Raich Carter.

What is now the traditional season curtain raiser was played on 28th October which was a Wednesday afternoon. The attendance of 11,500 was less than half the number who had seen the Black Cats beat West Bromwich Albion the previous Saturday.

The Black Cats had the better of the first half in which both sides were wasteful with their chances. Eight minutes after the restart, Eddie Burbanks atoned for three earlier missed chances when he gave Sunderland the lead. Arsenal then equalised with thirteen minutes remaining.

A minute from full time, Carter struck a fierce shot from the right that hit the bar and was cleared by a defender after bouncing down. The linesman flagged and after he was consulted by the referee, a goal was awarded.

After the game, discussion in the boardroom centred around the legitimacy of the goal. Three London journalists said it should not have stood, but the *Sunderland Daily Echo* correspondent declared that the linesman, who was by the corner flag, had a better view than anybody in the press box.

Sunderland competed in the Charity Shield again the following year, losing to Manchester City.

FACT 35
1937
THE FIRST FA CUP WIN

Sunderland won the FA Cup for the first time in 1936-37. They came from behind to beat Preston North End 3-1 in the final, in which more players were Scottish than English.

Sunderland beat Southampton, Luton, Swansea, Wolves and Millwall to reach the final. Both final managers were Scottish, as were twelve of the 22 players, including five of Sunderland's.

A minute before half time Frank O'Donnell put Preston ahead with a shot that Johnny Mapson in the Sunderland goal had no chance of saving. It looked like yet again the cup would elude Sunderland, who had such a proud league heritage.

In the second half the Black Cats were transformed. Half backs Charlie Thompson and Sandy McNab got forward more and this increased the confidence of the forwards. Within seven minutes Bobby Gurney had equalised with a header from a corner. Twenty minutes from time Raich Carter put them ahead, running through on goal to score despite offside appeals.

With five minutes remaining Eddie Burbanks sealed the victory with a brilliant shot from a tight angle. The game had been watched by King George V and his wife Queen Elizabeth, who presented the cup to Carter.

FACT 36

1939
JOHNNY COCHRANE LEAVES

Johnny Cochrane, the only manager to lead Sunderland to the Football League Championship and FA Cup, left the club in 1939.

Sunderland had needed a last day victory over Middlesbrough to avoid relegation when Cochrane replaced Bob Kyle in 1928. He instantly improved things, finishing fourth in his first season in charge.

Cochrane liked to mould players in the reserves before they were introduced to the first team. He was an excellent judge of a player and snapped up many bargains that served the club well before being sold for high fees.

This steady development paid off with the Black Cats reaching the semi-finals of the FA Cup in 1931 and then finishing sixth and second in the league prior to becoming champions in 1936.

The following year the Black Cats won the FA Cup for the first time, coming from behind to beat Preston North End 3-1 at Wembley. In 1938 they had another good cup run but went out in the semi-final and finished eighth in the league.

In 1938-39 Sunderland failed to meet their previous high standards and they were fourteenth at the end of February. It was still a surprise however when Cochrane resigned at the beginning of March even more so when he took over at Reading of the Third Division South just two weeks later.

FACT 37
1942
WAR CUP
RUNNERS UP

Sunderland gave their supporters some wartime cheer in 1942 when they reached the final of the Football League War Cup. However, they were beaten over two legs by Wolverhampton Wanderers.

With both the Football League and FA Cup suspended at the outbreak of war, regional competitions were organised on an ad hoc basis. With so many players in the armed forces, clubs were allowed to use guests. The Football League War Cup was introduced with early rounds taking place on a regional basis.

For the only time in the competition's history, the 1942 final was played over two legs. The first was at Roker Park on 23rd May and attracted a crowd of 34,776. Wolves led 1-0 at half time thanks to a goal from Dennis Westcott, but the Black Cats hit back in the second half to lead 2-1 through Raich Carter and Albert Stubbins, a guest who usually played for Newcastle. Three minutes from full time Westcott equalised for Wolves.

A train carrying Sunderland fans to the second leg was machine gunned by a German plane, but nobody was injured. In the game itself Wolves took a 2-0 lead but Carter's 58th minute goal gave Sunderland hope. However, the home side scored two more to win 4-1 and 6-3 on aggregate.

FACT 38
1943
ROKER PARK BOMBED

Like many other British cities, Sunderland was bombed during the Second World War. 276 civilians were killed and it was estimated that 90% of the buildings suffered damage in one form or another. These included Sunderland's Roker Park ground, which was hit by the Luftwaffe in 1943.

Roker Park's proximity to the shipyards meant it was always likely to be hit by a stray bomb. The device fell on the pitch, but the blast also damaged the roof of the grandstand. Another dropped behind the Roker End, destroying a small clubhouse. A passing policeman was also killed.

The estimated cost of the damage was up to £5,000. The club had to pay for drainage works and relaying of the turf before it could claim any money back from the War Damage Commission. As the raid occurred during the close season, fixtures were not affected.

Sunderland returned to action on the new pitch on 28th August, thrashing Leeds United 7-1 in the Football League North. They finished the season ninth in a fifty-team table, although the ad hoc nature of the competition meant their only fixtures were against clubs from Yorkshire and the North East.

FACT 39
1947
TOP SCORER LEAVES

Bobby Gurney, Sunderland's all-time leading goalscorer, left the club in 1947. A one club man, he had been there for 22 years since signing as a seventeen-year-old in 1925.

Gurney joined the Black Cats after Charlie Buchan spotted him playing amateur football for Bishop Auckland. He had to be patient waiting for his debut, in which he scored against West Ham United in a 3-2 defeat on 3rd April 1926.

For his first three seasons, Gurney partnered Dave Halliday who scored more goals than him. When Halliday joined Arsenal in 1929, Gurney stepped up and finished as Sunderland's leading scorer for the next seven seasons (the last of these was joint with Raich Carter).

Gurney's last competitive appearances were in 1938-39. By the end of that season he had played 390 times for the Black Cats, scoring 228 goals. This is a figure that has yet to be beaten and they included Sunderland's opening goal in the 1937 FA Cup final. During the Second World War Gurney remained contracted as a player and made occasional appearances up until 1944.

In 1947 Gurney was offered a third benefit game by Sunderland but he declined it. He opted to leave his coaching role and became the full-time manager of Horden Colliery Welfare in the Northern League.

FACT 40

1949
YEOVIL

Sunderland were involved in one of the greatest shocks in FA Cup history in a fourth round tie in 1948-49. They were beaten 2-1 by Yeovil Town on the Southern League club's notorious sloping pitch.

Yeovil had beaten fellow non-league clubs in the first two rounds, then in the third they caused an upset, knocking out Bury who were near the top of the Second Division.

The Black Cats were refused permission to train on the sloping pitch at the Huish. However, they were still expected to win comfortably, especially when Yeovil's first choice keeper had to drop out of the game due to a shoulder injury. His replacement had only made one appearance previously for the club so far.

In the first half Yeovil were the stronger side and deservedly took the lead after half an hour. Seventeen minutes into the second half Jackie Robinson equalised but neither side could find a winner. Due to fuel shortages, drawn cup ties then went to extra time.

As fog descended, Len Shackleton misplaced a pass allowing Yeovil to regain the lead. For the last fifteen minutes Sunderland dominated, their superior fitness telling. However, Yeovil held on for a famous victory, leaving the Black Cats humiliated. In the next round, Yeovil were drawn away to Manchester United and were thrashed 8-0.

FACT 41

1950
BANK OF ENGLAND CLUB
FINISHES THIRD

In the late 1940s and early 1950s Sunderland were commonly referred to as the 'Bank of England club'. However, despite spending vast sums on players, the highest finish they achieved was third in 1949-50.

Sunderland spent around £250,000 in the post war years. This included paying Newcastle a British record £20,050 for Len Shackleton in February 1948. That season the Black Cats finished just one place above the relegation zone but improved to finish eighth in 1948-49.

Despite the huge outlays, Sunderland's highest post war league position was third in 1949-50. They went top with five games remaining, only to lose three in succession and finish a point behind champions Portsmouth.

In an attempt to build on their third-place finish Sunderland broke the transfer record again. Welsh international Trevor Ford was signed from Aston Villa for £30,000. However, the Black Cats finished twelfth in the next two seasons. Ford and Shackleton never gelled on or off the pitch, with Ford even refusing to play on one occasion if Shackleton was in the team.

Shackleton later admitted that Sunderland's Bank of England approach had been a failure, as they were a collection of individuals rather than a team. The 1950s were a disappointing decade culminating in relegation in 1958.

FACT 42
1952
FLOODLIGHTS

In 1952 Sunderland became only the second club in England after Arsenal to install floodlights. They were switched on two weeks before Christmas for a friendly against Scottish Cup holders Dundee.

The lights at Roker Park were on top of four pylons, each 75 feet in height, erected at the four corners of the ground. Lighting was also installed in the stands and stairways to ensure spectator safety.

The friendly against Dundee attracted a crowd of over 34,000 which was lower than the league average but not significantly so. In order that the crowd could keep up with play, four match balls were used, meaning that they could be regularly switched and the mud cleaned off them.

In an entertaining game Arthur Wright gave Sunderland the lead after twenty minutes but Dundee hit back to lead 2-1 at half time. Trevor Ford equalised a minute into the second half and by the hour mark Sunderland led 4-2 thanks to a strike by Tommy Wright and another by Ford.

With twenty minutes remaining Dickie Davis got Sunderland's fifth. It finished 5-3, Dundee scoring a consolation five minutes from the end. The *Hartlepool Daily Mail* was impressed with the lights, reporting that "visibility was perfect and every incident crystal clear."

FACT 43
1957
LEN ASHURST SIGNS

Len Ashurst, who played more outfield games for Sunderland than any other player, signed for the club in 1957.

Ashurst was an eighteen-year-old apprentice printer playing for Prescot Cables in the Lancashire Combination. He joined the Black Cats in December 1957 but was used in the reserves that season and not thrown into the thick of a relegation battle.

Early in 1958-59 manager Alan Brown began to dismantle the side that had got relegated. Ashurst was one of three youngsters given their debuts against Ipswich Town at Roker Park on 20th September 1958. The Black Cats lost 2-0 but he impressed at full back and remained in the side for the rest of the season.

Ashurst made the left back position his own until the end of 1969-70, when he was granted a testimonial. He played a total of 458 games, was booked just thirteen times and was never sent off. He scored four goals for the club, but five own goals.

After Sunderland's relegation in 1970 he was given a free transfer and became player manager at Hartlepool. Fourteen years later he was back at Roker Park as manager in 1984, but he was not a success and was sacked following relegation the following year.

FACT 44

1958
RELEGATED FOR
THE FIRST TIME

In 1957-58 Sunderland were relegated for the first time in their history. In their 64th consecutive season in the topflight, they finished 21st and were relegated due to their inferior goal average.

Sunderland began the campaign with three straight defeats but recovered in early September with a win and two draws. For the first half of the season the Black Cats were perilously close to the bottom two, but it was in January when form really dipped.

On 8th March Sunderland blew a 3-1 lead at home to Sheffield Wednesday, who fought back to draw 3-3. This was their ninth game without a win, leaving them bottom of the table with nine games remaining. However, two wins and two draws lifted them up to nineteenth, meaning safety was in their own hands with five to go.

On Easter Saturday Sunderland suffered a humiliating 6-1 home defeat to Birmingham City. The next two games were also lost, leaving them needing a miracle to survive. Their last match was away to Portsmouth on 26th April. To avoid going down they needed a win and hope that Leicester City lost at Birmingham.

Although Sunderland won 2-0, Leicester also won and their amazing run of First Division seasons was over. This record of consecutive topflight seasons has since been broken by Arsenal and Everton.

FACT 45
1961
JIM MONTGOMERY
DEBUT

Sunderland's all-time record appearance holder is Jim Montgomery. The first of his 627 appearances for the Black Cats was in a League Cup second round tie against Walsall on 4th October 1961.

Montgomery was five days short of his eighteenth birthday when his chance came due to regular keeper Peter Wakeham having a fractured cheekbone. The Black Cats won 5-2 and Montgomery could do nothing about the goals he conceded, both of which came after errors by defenders.

The following night Montgomery was in action again, playing in the FA Youth Cup at Middlesbrough. Wakeham returned to the side for the next league game but in 1962-63 Montgomery became the Black Cats' first choice keeper.

Montgomery was promoted twice with Sunderland and was keeper for the famous 1973 FA Cup win. He made an incredible double save in the second half and was the first player to be embraced by manager Bob Stokoe after the game.

Early in 1976-77, as Sunderland struggled following promotion to the First Division, Barry Siddall was signed from Leicester and replaced Montgomery as the number one keeper. He remained in the topflight, signing for Birmingham City where he spent two seasons. He ended his career at Nottingham Forest where he won a European Cup winners medal in 1980 as an unused substitute.

FACT 46

1962
BRIAN CLOUGH'S CAREER ENDING INJURY

One of football's greatest managers, Brian Clough, saw his playing career brought to an end whilst with Sunderland. A cruciate ligament injury sustained in a game against Bury on Boxing Day led to him retiring from playing and managing a Football League club aged just thirty.

Sunderland paid £55,000 to Middlesbrough for Clough in 1961. He had been a prolific scorer there, scoring forty or more goals four seasons running.

The Boxing Day game with Bury at Roker Park was played on a treacherous pitch. It had been icy but was beginning to thaw and there was also torrential rain. In the 27th minute Clough was through on goal but collided with Bury's keeper. It resulted in torn ligaments and he didn't play again that season.

Clough remained out of action for the whole of 1963-64 and the following season managed just three games before deciding to end his playing career. He had scored 63 goals in 74 appearances for the Black Cats.

After a brief coaching role with Sunderland, Clough accepted the manager's job at Hartlepool in October 1965. Just seven months after his thirtieth birthday he was the youngest manager in the league. He went on to far greater things, leading Nottingham Forest to two European Cups.

FACT 47

1963
BLOWING PROMOTION

Sunderland looked all set for promotion in 1962-63. However, they lost their last game to Chelsea at Roker Park, who went up in their place.

A terrible winter meant that the Black Cats didn't play a single league game between 29th December and 23rd February. Although they had lost Brian Clough through injury, they remained in the promotion hunt.

At the end of March the Black Cats were top of the table, but in April they won only one in seven. This left them third with four games remaining. However, three straight wins meant a draw at home to Chelsea on 18th May would guarantee promotion.

The Black Cats had no intention of sitting back. They dominated the game for the first twenty minutes, forcing a number of good saves from keeper Peter Bonetti. After 25 minutes Chelsea scored from their first attack, Tommy Harmer diverting a low corner into the net to stun the home support. Sunderland were again the superior side in the second half but they couldn't find a goal.

The defeat meant the Black Cats were two points ahead of Chelsea, who still had one game left to play and a superior goal average. The following Tuesday at Stamford Bridge, Chelsea made no mistake. They thrashed Portsmouth 7-0 and condemned Sunderland to another season in the Second Division.

1964
AWAY FORM TAKES SUNDERLAND UP

FACT 48

Sunderland did manage to get promoted back to the First Division in 1963-64. They went up partly due to their splendid away form, losing just four games on the road.

In their seventh game Sunderland beat Manchester City 2-0 at Roker Park to move into the top two and they remained there all season. 26 of their 61 points were gained away from home as they battled all the way with Leeds United for top spot. They eventually finished a point behind Leeds, but five ahead of third placed Preston North End.

Going into the penultimate game of the season, at home to Charlton Athletic, the Black Cats needed just a point to guarantee promotion. They were desperate to do so in front of their own fans as the last game was at Grimsby Town.

In front of a huge crowd of 50,827 Charlton's Eddie Firmani stunned the home support with a goal after seventeen minutes. Sunderland were below par but two minutes before half time George Herd's shot deflected over the keeper to level the scores.

Charlton had to play most of the second half with ten men and rarely looked like spoiling the party. With a minute to go Johnny Crossan hit an unstoppable shot to send the crowd wild as they returned to the topflight after six years away.

FACT 49
1964
SUNDERLAND'S YOUNGEST PLAYER

On 22nd August 1964 a goalkeeping crisis at Sunderland meant that teenager Derek Forster was given his debut. He was just 15 years and 185 years old.

It was the opening day of the new season and Sunderland were back in the First Division after six years. However, a few days before the game regular keeper Jim Montgomery injured his left hand.

It was widely assumed that regular reserve keeper Derek Kirby would step up, or there would be a late move into the transfer market. Instead, Forster was selected despite his young age and having only been with the club a month.

Forster, who had played in front of 95,000 at Wembley for England schoolboys, didn't put a foot wrong. He could not be faulted for any of the goals he conceded as the Black Cats drew 3-3 with Leicester City at Roker Park. In the other goal was Gordon Banks, a future World Cup winner with England.

An attempt to bring former Manchester City keeper Bert Trautmann out of retirement failed, meaning Forster kept his place whilst Montgomery recovered from injury. However, he made only eighteen appearances in total for the club and eventually left for Charlton Athletic in 1973.

Forster continues to hold the record of youngest player in Sunderland's history, as well as the youngest in England's topflight.

FACT 50
1966
THE WORLD CUP

Sunderland hosted some of the biggest names in football in 1966. Roker Park was a venue for three group stage games in the World Cup, but crowds were still lower than for most First Division games.

Along with Middlesbrough's Ayresome Park, Roker Park was chosen as one of two North East venues for the tournament. They hosted games in Group D, which consisted of Italy, Chile, North Korea and the USSR.

The first game at Roker Park was on 13th July between Italy and Chile. Sandro Mazzola, twice a European Cup winner with Inter Milan and Serie A top scorer in 1964-65, was on target as the Italians won 2-0. Three days later Italy faced the USSR, who had the legendary Lev Yashin in goal. He kept a clean sheet in a 1-0 victory that secured a place in the quarter finals.

Both games involving Italy were watched by crowds of over 27,000. The final group game at Roker Park between the USSR and Chile, attracted far less interest with just over 16,000 present to see the USSR win 2-1.

Roker Park then hosted a quarter final between USSR and Hungary, which USSR won 2-1 in front of a crowd of just under 27,000. In contrast, Sunderland had averaged 33,000 during the season, the lowest attendance being 20,108.

FACT 51
1967 VANCOUVER ROYAL CANADIANS

In 1967 Sunderland took part in a summer league in North America. They were rebranded the Vancouver Royal Canadians and played twelve games in the Western Division of the United Soccer Association.

Sunderland/Vancouver were based at the Empire Stadium, venue for the 1954 Commonwealth Games. The other teams in their division were Los Angeles Wolves (Wolverhampton Wanderers), San Francisco Golden Gate Gales (ADO Den Haag), Chicago Mustangs (Cagliari), Dallas Tornado (Dundee United) and Houston Stars (Bangu).

The format saw Sunderland playing twelve games over the season, which ran from 28th May to 8th July. They played members of their own division once and also a game against the six teams of the Eastern Division. They met the other Canadian based team (Toronto City/Hibernian) both home and away.

The competition was not universally popular, with Sunderland's 'home' games attracting an average crowd of just 7,019. Sunderland won just three of their twelve games, finishing fifth in their division. This at least meant they didn't have to stay another week to play the final, with their first pre-season campaign beginning on 5th August.

FACT 52

1969
PLAYER OF
THE CENTURY

Charlie Hurley, voted Sunderland's 'Player of the Century' during their centenary celebrations, left the club in 1969. The Irish centre back made 401 appearances for the Black Cats, scoring a respectable 26 goals.

Hurley was twenty years old and already an international when he joined the Black Cats from Millwall early in the 1957-58 season. His first two games ended in 7-0 and 6-0 defeats, but things improved considerably from there.

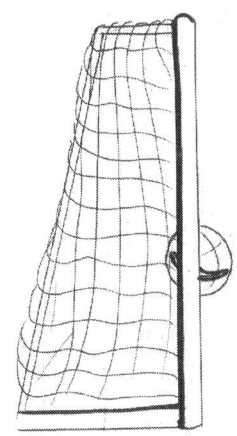

When the Black Cats won promotion in 1964, Hurley was voted the Football Writers Player of the Year. It took him three years to score his first goal for the club, a second half equaliser against Sheffield United on Boxing Day 1960. This was the first of 26 for the club, many of them powerful headers.

Hurley was a great header, tackler and had excellent ball control. His versatility meant he even deputised in goal in a match against Manchester United in 1966 when Jim Montgomery went off injured.

In 1969 Hurley was given a free transfer by Sunderland and joined Second Division Bolton Wanderers. Ten years later during the club's centenary he was voted their player of the century. When his biography was published in 2008 by Sunderland historian Mark Metcalf, it was titled *The Greatest Centre Half The World Has Ever Seen*.

FACT 53

1970
RELEGATED

Sunderland were relegated for only the second time in their history in 1969-70. It was a woeful season in which they won just six games and were rarely out of the bottom two.

The Black Cats failed to win any of their first eleven games and didn't score a goal until their fifth. It was clearly in attack where the problem was and they managed just thirty goals all season. Top scorer was Gordon Harris with seven, four of them penalties.

Apart from a few weeks in January, the Black Cats remained in the relegation zone all season. Too many games were drawn and at Roker Park they won just four times. One of those victories was a 2-1 win over Ipswich Town that attracted a pitiful crowd of just 12,739.

Despite such a dire season, Sunderland still had survival in their own hands going into their last game of the season. Victory over Liverpool would ensure they would stay up and send Crystal Palace down.

It was an end-to-end game and the Black Cats had their fair share of attacks. However, Liverpool's experienced defence was easily able to handle their shot shy attack. With four minutes remaining Chris Lawler scored for Liverpool and confirmed Sunderland would be joining Sheffield Wednesday in the Second Division the following season.

FACT 54
1970
ANGLO ITALIAN CUP

Sunderland took part in the inaugural Anglo Italian Cup in 1970. They were eliminated in the group stage and didn't compete in it again.

The competition was set up to help clubs generate an income during the extended close season caused by the World Cup. Sunderland's last league game had been on 15th April and the Anglo Italian Cup ran throughout May.

Twelve teams were split into three groups of four, with two English and two Italian sides in each. The English and Italian teams played each other home and away. All results were then pooled together and the teams from each country with the best records met in a two legged final.

Sunderland's fans were underwhelmed by the competition. Just 3,764 attended the 3-1 home win over Lazio but this rose to 5,967 for the game with Fiorentina, which was drawn 2-2.

The squad then spent a week in Italy, losing their first game against Lazio 3-1 in Rome. The Black Cats then beat Perugia 2-1 in a friendly before moving on to Florence to play Fiorentina, losing 3-0.

Sunderland finished fifth in the table of English teams and did not take part in any of the next three tournaments before it was abandoned altogether. They did compete in the 1990s however, when it involved all second-tier clubs from both countries.

FACT 55
1973
SUNDERLAND STUN
LEEDS IN CUP FINAL

In 1973 Sunderland caused one of the greatest shocks in FA Cup final history. They beat hot favourites Leeds United 1-0 at Wembley to lift the trophy for the second time.

Sunderland had endured a difficult league season. A nine-game winless run in the autumn saw them drop to the brink of the relegation zone, but after Christmas they improved and eventually finished sixth. This was coupled with a run in the cup that saw them defeat First Division Manchester City and Arsenal on their way to the final.

Leeds were the cup holders and had finished second to Liverpool in the league table. However, the Black Cats refused to be overawed and held their own for the opening half hour. In the 31st minute from a corner the ball bounced fortunately to Ian Porterfield, who fired it into the net from just outside the six-yard box.

In the second half Sunderland faced sustained spells of pressure. Keeper Jim Montgomery made one superb double save, parrying a header from Trevor Cherry then pushing Peter Lorimer's follow up shot onto the bar.

At full time Sunderland manager Bob Stokoe ran onto the pitch and embraced his keeper. Sunderland had pulled off what many thought was impossible and become the first club from the Second Division to win the FA Cup since 1931.

FACT 56
1973
EUROPE

Sunderland's only appearance in European competition was in 1973-74. They qualified for the European Cup Winners Cup as FA Cup holders but were beaten in the second round.

In the first round, Sunderland had to travel behind the Iron Curtain to face Hungarian side Vasas. They won 2-0 in Budapest thanks to second half goals from Billy Hughes and Dennis Tueart. In the return at Roker Park, raised admission prices and weather meant a disappointing crowd of 22,762 who saw Tueart's penalty complete a 3-0 aggregate victory.

The Black Cats were drawn at home to Portuguese giants Sporting Lisbon in the second round, with the first leg at home. Goals from Bobby Kerr and Micky Horswill put Sunderland in control but Sporting's Hector Yazalde scored a crucial away goal five minutes from full time.

After 26 minutes of the second leg Yazalde put Sporting ahead on away goals. It came about from a terrible mistake by Sunderland keeper Jim Montgomery, who threw the ball to him. In the second half Samuel Fraguito scored another for Sporting who went through 3-2 on aggregate. Sunderland have not played in Europe since.

1974 TEXACO CUP

Sunderland's only appearance in the Texaco Cup, a sponsored tournament that ran for five years in the early 1970s, was in 1974-75.

The competition was one of the first sponsored tournaments in the world. It was open to clubs from the British Isles who had not qualified for European competition and carried a prize fund of £100,000 which was a considerable sum at the time.

The regional group stage of the competition took place prior to the start of the regular season. Sunderland were alongside Newcastle, Middlesbrough and Carlisle United.

Sunderland's opening game against Newcastle at Roker Park attracted a healthy crowd of over 28,000. The Black Cats won 2-1 thanks to goals from Vic Halom and Bobby Kerr. They then lost 1-0 at home to Middlesbrough and could only draw 0-0 at Carlisle. This meant they failed to progress to the knockout stage and the chance of a game against Scottish opposition.

Newcastle went on to win the competition that year. Texaco then ended their sponsorship and it was rebranded the Anglo Scottish Cup for 1975-76. Sunderland took part in the Anglo Scottish Cup three times but never made it out of the group stages.

FACT 58

1976
SECOND DIVISION
CHAMPIONS

Sunderland won promotion as Second Division Champions in 1975-76. In a memorable season, they were unbeaten at Roker Park, winning nineteen of their 21 matches.

A 2-0 victory at home to West Bromwich Albion in their seventh game lifted Sunderland into the promotion positions. They remained for the rest of the season, most of it in first or second place.

The Roker Roar was a major factor. Sunderland averaged nearly 33,000 over the season and only the two Bristol clubs, City and Rovers, came away with a point.

On Easter Monday the Black Cats faced Bolton Wanderers at Roker Park, knowing a win would secure promotion with two games remaining. In front of a huge crowd of 51,893 Tony Towers gave Sunderland the lead from the penalty spot after half an hour. Seven minutes later Pop Robson doubled the lead when he turned in a Bobby Kerr cross.

With twelve minutes remaining Sam Allardyce headed home for Bolton, keeping alive their own promotion hopes. It meant a nervous end to the game for the home fans but the Black Cats held on. Fans swarmed the pitch at the end to mob their heroes, back in the First Division.

Sunderland lost their penultimate game 1-0 at Blackpool then wrapped up the championship with a 2-0 home win over Portsmouth in their final game.

FACT 59

1976
BOB STOKOE
RESIGNS

After failing to win any of the first nine games of the 1976-77 season, Sunderland's manager Bob Stokoe shocked the club by resigning.

Stokoe, who played over 400 games for Newcastle, had been appointed in November 1972 when the Black Cats were nineteenth in the Second Division. He steered them to a sixth-place finish and glory in the FA Cup.

Sunderland just missed out on promotion in the next two seasons. Stokoe even tendered his resignation, but the board remained confident in him. In 1975-76 they went up as champions, but Stokoe was dogged by ill health and missed several games due to migraines. He opted not to go on the club's summer tour of Australia and the Far East, instead taking a well-earned holiday.

Stokoe returned tanned and refreshed ready for the new season. However, despite splashing out £400,000 on four new players, the Black Cats made a disastrous start and didn't win any of their first nine games. It was still a shock that Stokoe decided to quit, especially as he left without even saying goodbye to the players.

Seven weeks later, Stokoe gave a radio interview saying he needed to give the players a fresh start. Today his achievements are honoured at the Stadium of Light where there is a statue of him.

FACT 60
1977
RELEGATED THANKS TO A DELAYED KICKOFF

Sunderland were relegated straight back to the Second Division in 1976-77. They went down when two teams played out a draw knowing it would keep them both up at Sunderland's expense.

After Bob Stokoe's resignation, caretaker boss Ian McFarlane oversaw a slight improvement. However, after Jimmy Adamson was appointed at the end of November they didn't win until his tenth game. This 1-0 home win over Bristol City was the first of four straight wins that lifted Sunderland out of the relegation zone.

By the last game, the Black Cats knew what they needed to do. A win or draw away to Everton would guarantee survival, as they had a better goal difference than Coventry and Bristol City who were playing each other at Highfield Road.

Sunderland's game kicked off on time, but at Highfield Road, Coventry's managing director Jimmy Hill delayed kick off by ten minutes, citing congestion outside the ground. Sunderland lost 2-0, meaning they would be down if the other game was drawn.

When it was announced that Sunderland had lost, it was 2-2 at Highfield Road. The closing stages were played out in farcical fashion, with Bristol City's defenders passing the ball amongst themselves most of the time. Coventry were later reprimanded for the delayed kick-off, but the result stood.

FACT 61
1979
GARY ROWELL'S
DERBY HAT TRICK

Sunderland's 4-1 victory over Newcastle at St James Park on 24th February 1979 was particularly memorable for Gary Rowell. He scored a hat trick, the first by a Sunderland player in the fixture for 65 years.

Rowell's first goal after seven minutes was a scrambled effort from six yards after the ball was pumped into the box. Midway through the first half he finished coolly after latching on to a brilliant long ball.

Early in the second half Johnny Connolly's header gave hope to the home side. Soon after the hour mark, the Black Cats were awarded a penalty and Rowell stepped forward to send the keeper the wrong way with his kick. Wayne Entwistle completed the scoring with eleven minutes remaining.

This was the first time a Sunderland player had scored a hat trick in the derby at St James Park since Bobby Best did so in a 5-2 victory in 1915. Afterwards, 21-year-old Rowell was extremely modest, pointing out that one of his goals was a penalty. He admitted that it was his proudest day in football but scoring just once in a victory was enough.

Rowell remained at Sunderland until 1984. He now works as a radio summariser and was voted best player of the 1980s by fanzine *A Love Supreme* in 2006.

FACT 62
1979
CENTENARY YEAR

Sunderland celebrated their centenary in the autumn and winter of 1979 with events commemorating the first 100 years of the club.

On 7th November Roker Park hosted a centenary celebration match between Sunderland and an England XI. Prior to kick off, there was a parade of ex Black Cats stars including two surviving members of the 1937 FA Cup winning side — Bobby Gurney and Johnny Mapson.

When the game started the England XI, containing a number of players hoping to earn a full international call up, were by far the better side. They won 2-0 thanks to a headed goal in each half from Bob Latchford. The game had been played on a Wednesday night and attracted a crowd of 11,739 which was less than half that season's average.

The Sunderland AFC Centenary Banquet took place on 25th November at the Mayfair Ballroom. Television personality Frank Bough was the host and guests included the Mayor of Sunderland and Vice President of the Football Association. Gurney was present again, as was 1973 FA Cup winning manager Bob Stokoe. Charlie Hurley was acknowledged as player of the century by the supporters' association.

It was activities on the pitch that interested the supporters most however. By the end of the season, the centenary had been a perfect one as the Black Cats won promotion to the First Division.

FACT 63
1980
PROMOTED IN CENTENARY SEASON

Sunderland enjoyed a perfect end to their centenary season in 1979-80. They beat West Ham United 2-0 at Roker Park to secure a return to the First Division.

A victory at Cardiff City on the last day of the regular season, 3rd May, would guarantee promotion. However, despite Sunderland's fans making up more than half of the crowd, they could only draw 1-1. It meant an agonising wait until 12th May, when Sunderland knew a draw against West Ham United at Roker Park would see them leapfrog Chelsea into the promotion places.

A crowd of 47,129 squeezed into Roker Park, with thousands more locked out. West Ham had shocked Arsenal two days earlier to win the FA Cup final but were in no mood to relax and had the better chances in the opening half hour.

After forty minutes the crowd's nerves were eased when Kevin Arnott scored after the keeper had kept out efforts from Pop Robson and Shaun Elliot. In the 72nd minute Stan Cummins settled things when he took the ball past three men before unleashing an unstoppable shot from twenty yards.

After the game manager Ken Knighton sipped champagne in the dressing room and told reporters, "We have deserved this over the season." The players were then rewarded with a well-earned break in Miami.

FACT 64

1981
LAST DAY
SURVIVAL

Sunderland avoided relegation straight back to the Second Division in dramatic fashion in 1980-81. On the last day of the season, they had a rare win at Liverpool thanks to a first half goal from Stan Cummins.

In the middle of November the Black Cats looked to be comfortable in mid table. They then won just one out of eight to drop to seventeenth. Although they never fell into the relegation zone all season, they were still not safe by the final game and faced a three-way fight with Brighton and Norwich City to stay up.

To guarantee survival they needed to beat Liverpool at Anfield, where they had failed to win in 22 league games, going back to 1936. The other two clubs in danger were both at home, with Norwich City hosting already relegated Leicester City.

Sunderland were nervous early on, but their huge travelling support let them know Norwich were losing and this increased their confidence. After 31 minutes Cummins rounded off a fine move with a fierce left foot shot from just inside the area.

In the second half Sunderland had a few early chances to double their lead but tired and Liverpool took control. Keeper Barry Siddall and Sunderland's defence kept battling to hold on for a famous victory and avoid the drop.

65
1985
TWO RELEGATED SIDES IN LEAGUE CUP FINAL

Sunderland lost the 1984-85 League Cup final which made history for the wrong reasons. It was the only occasion when a domestic cup final was contested by two sides who were relegated that season.

Sunderland had a tough route to the final, facing topflight opposition from the third round onwards. Their scalps included Tottenham Hotspur, who were challenging for the title. Norwich City, on the other hand, didn't play a First Division side until the semi-final.

David Hodgson almost put the Black Cats ahead in the first minute but his dipping shot went just over the bar. Norwich had the better of the first half and it remained 0-0 at half time.

Within a minute of the restart, Sunderland's David Corner was dispossessed whilst trying to usher the ball out for a goal kick. The ball fell to Asa Hartford whose shot deflected off Gordon Chisholm into the net.

Three minutes after Norwich scored, Sunderland were awarded a penalty for handball. Clive Walker's kick came back off the post and they were unable to find an equaliser. At the end it was a sporting occasion, with Sunderland's fans applauding the Norwich players as they paraded the trophy.

There was still a quarter of the league season to go, but both saw a downturn in fortunes and dropped into the Second Division in May.

FACT 66
1985 RELEGATION AFTER CUP FINAL

Sunderland never recovered from losing the League Cup final in 1984-85. They won just one of their last twelve games and were relegated to the Second Division.

At the beginning of November, Sunderland were seventh in the table, but soon began to lose form. The League Cup run though somewhat distracted eyes from the league table, as they fell into the bottom six.

A week after the Wembley defeat, Sunderland lost 2-0 to Chelsea at Roker Park, then 3-0 at home to Liverpool a few days later. Next, they lost 4-1 at champions-elect Everton before a drab Easter Monday derby at home to Newcastle was drawn 0-0. This meant Sunderland fell into the bottom three for the first time that season, with eight games remaining.

Sunderland lifted themselves out of the relegation zone with a crucial win at Coventry City, but they then failed to win any of their last seven games. New signings had failed to gel, youth players were given a chance too early and manager Len Ashurst simply couldn't find a way out of the situation.

Relegation was confirmed in the penultimate game when Sunderland lost 2-0 at Leicester City. The season then ended with a 2-1 home defeat to Ipswich Town, watched by a crowd of just 9,398.

1987
DOWN TO
THE THIRD DIVISION

FACT 67

Sunderland were relegated to the third tier of English football for the first time in their history in 1986-87. After finishing third from bottom of the Second Division, they lost a two-legged play-off with Gillingham.

Although Sunderland struggled all season, they didn't fall into the bottom three until April. They knew that victory in their last game of the season at home to Barnsley would guarantee survival and keep them out of the dreaded play-off s.

After half an hour the Black Cats were leading 2-0 but a Barnsley goal two minutes from half time changed the atmosphere. Mark Proctor missed a penalty after an hour and the visitors then struck twice to win 3-2. With Shrewsbury Town beating Birmingham City, it condemned Sunderland to a play-off semi-final with Gillingham, who had finished sixth in the Third Division.

Sunderland lost the first leg at Priestfield 3-2. Back at Roker Park, Proctor again missed a penalty when the home side led 2-1. Gillingham equalised but Gary Bennett scored with two minutes remaining to force extra time.

Tony Cascarino's strike in the 93rd minute meant Gillingham now had the away goals advantage. Although Keith Bertschin made it 4-3 in the second period, Sunderland couldn't find a fifth goal and they dropped into the Third Division.

FACT 68

1988
THIRD DIVISION
CHAMPIONS

Sunderland's first stay in the Third Division was a short one. After a shaky start they went straight back up as champions, finishing eleven points clear of the play-off positions.

September was a bad month for Sunderland as they went five without a win to fall to twelfth. However, a 2-0 win at Fulham on 29th September was the first of six straight victories that lifted them to the top by the end of October. They remained in the promotion positions all season.

Key to this rise was new signing Marco Gabbiadini. The nineteen-year-old signed from York City was an instant success. He formed a great strike partnership with Eric Gates, with the pair scoring forty goals between them.

Between November and February Sunderland enjoyed a fourteen-game unbeaten run. This included a 7-0 thrashing of Southend United at Roker Park in which Gates scored four. Even a spell of four without a win in March was only delaying the inevitable.

On 29th April, Gates scored the only goal as Sunderland won 1-0 at Port Vale, securing promotion with two games remaining. Two days later 29,454 at Roker Park saw them clinch the championship with a 3-1 win over Northampton Town. They finished the season with 93 points, eleven ahead of Walsall in third.

FACT 69

1990
AN EXTRAORDINARY PROMOTION

Sunderland went up in extraordinary circumstances in 1989-90. They lost the play-off final but were then promoted when their opponents Swindon Town were found guilty of financial irregularities.

Throughout the season Sunderland rarely looked likely to challenge for the top two but they were always there or thereabouts for the play-off places. They eventually finished sixth, setting up a play-off semi-final with Newcastle United.

They were undoubtedly the most important games in the history of the Tyne-Wear derby. At Roker Park the two sides drew 0-0, then at St James Park goals from Eric Gates and Marco Gabbiadini took Sunderland to the final.

For the first time, the play-off final was a single game played at Wembley. The Black Cats started well and missed two chances in the first five minutes, but Swindon soon took control of the game. In the 23rd minute Alan McLaughlin's strike deflected off Gary Bennett to give the Wiltshire side the lead. They dominated the rest of the game and Sunderland were lucky only to lose 1-0.

Ten days after the final, Swindon were found guilty of irregular payments to players. They were demoted to the Third Division, but this was later reduced to the Second Division on appeal. It meant however that Sunderland would play in the First Division for 1990-91.

FACT 70

1991
STRAIGHT BACK DOWN

Sunderland's return to the First Division was brief but they left with their heads held high. They went down on a tense last day of the season, backed by 15,000 of their fans at Manchester City.

Going into the final game Sunderland were level on points with Luton Town with the same goal difference, so had to better their result to stay up. Luton were at home to Derby County, while Sunderland were at a side who were fifth in the table.

There were 15,000 Sunderland fans at Maine Road who saw City take an early lead through Niall Quinn. Marco Gabbiadini levelled with a header five minutes before half time, then a minute before the break Gary Bennett put Sunderland ahead. Quinn then scored an immediate equaliser.

In the second half the Black Cats couldn't find a winning goal, then were deflated to hear that Luton were 2-0 up. With a minute left, Sunderland's relegation was confirmed when David White scored for City.

After the final whistle, most of Sunderland's support, many of them in fancy dress, remained behind. They refused to leave until manager Denis Smith and his players came back out to applaud them 45 minutes later. They may not have been good enough on the pitch, but off it Sunderland fans had set a fine example.

FACT 71
1992
FA CUP FINALISTS

Sunderland enjoyed a memorable run to the FA Cup final in 1991-92. However, there was to be no fairy tale ending as they were beaten 2-0 by Liverpool at Wembley.

Back in the Second Division, the Black Cats failed to mount a promotion push. Denis Smith resigned shortly after Christmas and his assistant, Malcolm Crosby, took over as manager.

In the third round of the cup, Sunderland enjoyed a comfortable 3-0 victory over Port Vale at Roker Park. They then won 3-2 at Oxford United and were drawn at home to topflight West Ham United in the fifth round. After a 1-1 draw, Sunderland caused an upset by winning the replay 3-2 at Upton Park.

Sunderland were drawn away to Chelsea in the sixth round, drawing 1-1 at Stamford Bridge then winning the replay 2-1. In the semi-final Sunderland faced First Division opposition for the third time. John Byrne's 34th minute goal against Norwich City at Hillsborough was enough to take them to the final.

Despite being underdogs the Black Cats had the better of Liverpool in the first half and Byrne miskicked when he had a great chance from six yards. Early in the second half Michael Thomas scored for Liverpool and Ian Rush doubled their lead after 68 minutes. The game finished 2-0 and Sunderland haven't reached the final since.

FACT 72
1996
PROMOTED TO
THE PREMIER LEAGUE

After a battle with relegation in 1994-95, Sunderland were transformed the following season. They finished as champions of the First Division (the name for the second tier since 1992) to gain promotion to the Premier League for the first time.

With Sunderland fighting the drop in March 1995, Mick Buxton was sacked and Peter Reid appointed temporarily. He steered the club to safety and was given the manager's job permanently in time for the 1995-96 season.

The Black Cats had a mixed start, but after ten games were in the play-off positions. A 6-0 win over Millwall at Roker Park on 9th December took them to the top of the table but they then won just one from nine and fell to fifth.

On 20th February Sunderland won 1-0 at home to Ipswich Town, the first of nine successive wins that returned them to the top. After beating Birmingham City 3-0 at Roker Park on 16th April, the Black Cats needed just one point from three games to secure promotion.

Four days later Birmingham drew 1-1 at Derby County, meaning Sunderland went up without kicking a ball. The following day at Roker Park there was a carnival atmosphere for the game with Stoke City, which ended 0-0. Sunderland ended the season as champions with 83 points, twelve clear of third place Crystal Palace.

FACT 73
1997 FINAL DAY RELEGATION

As Sunderland prepared to move to a new 42,000 seat stadium, they were unable to ensure it would be hosting Premier League football. After making a promising start to the 1996-97 season, they were relegated on the final day.

Sunderland were unbeaten in their first three games. These included an impressive 4-1 win at Nottingham Forest and 0-0 draw away to title hopefuls Liverpool. At New Year they were eleventh and looked to have adapted well to the Premier League.

A run of four straight defeats starting in February took the Black Cats closer to the relegation zone. Lack of squad depth and experience at this level was beginning to tell.

The Black Cats didn't fall into the bottom three until 13th April, when Liverpool won 2-1 at Roker Park. There were four games to go but a crucial 1-0 win at fellow strugglers Middlesbrough, followed by a 3-0 win over Everton in the last league game at Roker Park, meant survival was in their own hands on the last day.

Over 10,000 Sunderland fans headed to south London for the last game, knowing a win against Wimbledon at Selhurst Park would guarantee survival. It was a nervy performance and a late Jason Euell goal won it for Wimbledon. This, coupled with Coventry's win at Tottenham, condemned Sunderland to relegation.

FACT 74
1997
FAREWELL TO ROKER PARK

Sunderland left their home of 99 years in 1997. Due to the impact of the Taylor Report, Roker Park's limitations meant the club had to look elsewhere if they were to compete in the Premier League era.

Following the Hillsborough Disaster of 1989 when 96 Liverpool fans were crushed to death in an FA Cup semi-final, the Taylor Report recommended that stadiums become all seated. Government legislation then made this a requirement for the top two divisions.

Roker Park's capacity was already down to 22,500 and would decrease even further if converted to all seats. There was limited room for expansion and as early as 1992 the club considered a move, but the proposed site in Washington was opposed by car giants Nissan.

Instead, the club opted to build a 42,000 seat stadium at the disused Monkwearmouth colliery, close to the old Newcastle Road ground. 1996-97 would be the last season at Roker Park.

The last league game at Roker was on 3rd May, with Sunderland winning 3-0 to give themselves hope of avoiding relegation. Ten days later, another capacity crowd at Sunderland welcomed Liverpool, the first opponents at the ground, for a friendly. John Mullin scored the only goal in a 1-0 victory. Afterwards the centre circle was dug up and replanted at the new stadium.

FACT 75
1997
THE STADIUM OF LIGHT

Sunderland had a new home for the 1997-98 season. The impressive Stadium of Light had an all-seated capacity of 42,000.

After the planned development at Washington fell through, the club moved quickly to secure a deal to build on the site of the Monkwearmouth colliery, which closed in 1993. Initially the projected capacity was 34,000 but this rose to 42,000 during the construction process.

Little over eighteen months after the plans were approved by the Tyne and Wear Development Corporation, the new stadium was ready in July 1997. The name reflects the site's mining origins and a Davy lamp monument is situated there.

The stadium was officially opened by the Duke of York on 30th July. Bands including Upside Down and Status Quo performed before the Black Cats played a friendly against Ajax, winners of the Champions League two years earlier. They more than held their own in a 0-0 draw.

Three years after it opened the capacity was expanded to 49,000 and there is potential for further increase to 63,000. It has hosted three full England internationals and a number of high-profile pop concerts.

FACT 76
1998
PREMIER PASSIONS

Sunderland were the subject of a six part BBC documentary series broadcast in the Spring of 1998. Premier Passions chartered the second half of the 1996-97 season that ultimately ended in relegation.

Each episode was 45 minutes long and aired in chronological order. Narrated by actress and Sunderland fan Gina McKee, a common theme throughout was the search for a new striker that could score the goals to help the club escape relegation.

The series was unprecedented in terms of access given to the television crews. Half time team talks were filmed, which gained the most notoriety in the series due to manager Peter Reid's frequent use of swear words.

The boardroom also featured regularly, with discussions over the move to the Stadium of Light and floating of the club on the stock market. Fans involved came from a cross section of society and the series brought local fame to many of the participants, including groundsman Tommy Porter.

In August 1999, a one-off sequel was broadcast, Premier Pressure. This was aired a few days before the start of the new season, which saw Sunderland back in the Premier League and covered the pre-season preparations.

FACT 77
1998
PLAY-OFF FINAL
PENALTIES HEARTBREAK

Sunderland enjoyed a memorable first season at the Stadium of Light. However, they were unable to cap it with promotion as they lost the play-off final on penalties.

After a topsy turvy start, the Black Cats started to hit form from the middle of October. A 3-1 win over Huddersfield in their eleventh game was the start of a sixteen-game unbeaten run that lifted them into the play-off positions.

With two games to go promotion was in Sunderland's own hands but they lost the penultimate game 2-0 at Ipswich Town. They had to settle for the play-offs and overcame a first leg deficit against Sheffield United to win 2-0 at the Stadium of Light and 3-2 on aggregate.

Against Charlton Athletic at Wembley, Sunderland were roared on by 40,000 fans. It was a classic game for the neutral, as Sunderland came from behind to lead 2-1 and 3-2 only for Charlton to equalise five minutes from full time. Sunderland again led in extra time but were pegged back to 4-4.

All ten regular kicks in the penalty shoot-out were converted, meaning sudden death. Each side converted their sixth but when Michael Gray stepped up needing to score, he had the agony of seeing his kick saved and the Black Cats faced another year in the second tier.

FACT 78
1999
PROMOTED WITH A RECORD POINTS HAUL

After the heartbreak of losing a play-off final, Sunderland made no mistake in 1998-99. They finished the season with 105 points as they wrapped up promotion with four games to spare.

The Black Cats started the season with an eighteen-game unbeaten run and they remained top from October onwards. Even the loss of key striker Kevin Phillips for three months didn't stop the momentum. The first game in which he was absent, at home to Oxford United, was won 7-0 with his replacement Michael Bridges scoring twice.

On 30th January Sunderland were beaten 2-1 at Watford, their third defeat of the season. They responded with ten wins and two draws from the next twelve games to open up an insurmountable gap.

The inevitable promotion was confirmed on 13th April when the Black Cats beat Bury 5-2 at Gigg Lane. Phillips continued to make up for his injury absence by netting four of the goals and would end the season with a return of 23 from 26 games. At the back, Tommy Sorensen kept an amazing 29 clean sheets.

Sunderland didn't rest up and picked up ten points from their last four games. They finished eighteen clear of second placed Bradford City with 105 points, a second tier record at the time.

FACT 79
1999
A MOMENTOUS DERBY WIN

Sunderland came from behind to beat Newcastle at St James Park on 25th August 1999. It was their first topflight away win in the Tyne-Wear derby for 33 years and cost Newcastle manager Ruud Gullit his job.

Despite the game being played on a summer evening, the weather was atrocious, with the players battling heavy rain. Kieron Dyer gave Newcastle the lead after 27 minutes, lifting the ball over Tommy Sorensen as he tried to close the striker down.

The Black Cats continued battling and were rewarded on 64 minutes when Niall Quinn equalised with a glancing header from a Nicky Summerbee free kick.

With seventeen minutes remaining, Newcastle's star man Alan Shearer, surprisingly left out of the starting line-up, was brought off the bench. However, within two minutes Kevin Phillips scored a superb goal, lobbing the keeper from a tight angle after his first effort had been saved.

In injury time Sunderland's captain Kevin Ball almost scored a sensational own goal when his back pass from thirty yards came off the bar. Sunderland held out for a famous victory, while Newcastle's fans let their anger known at just one point from their first five matches.

The result cost Gullit his job. Sunderland enjoyed a fine season in the Premier League, harbouring dreams of European qualification for much of it. They eventually finished seventh.

FACT 80
2000 GOLDEN BOOT FOR KEVIN PHILLIPS

Kevin Phillips was sensational in his first season as a Premier League striker. He scored thirty league goals, winning the competition's Golden Boot and Europe's Golden Shoe.

Phillips had shown he could score goals in the First Division, netting sixty in two seasons since joining Sunderland. However, some pundits suggested he would struggle to step up to the higher level.

On Sky Sports, Rodney Marsh predicted that he would only get six goals. Phillips made a mockery of this and reached that figure after just eight games. As well as hitting a hat trick away to Derby County, he netted twice on eight other occasions, including three games in succession before Christmas.

Phillips formed a lethal partnership with Niall Quinn, who got fourteen himself. The Black Cats finished seventh, just missing out on European qualification. Phillips' thirty goals earned him the Golden Boot in addition to UEFA's Golden Shoe, having scored more than anyone in Europe's top leagues.

In each of his six seasons with Sunderland, Phillips was the club's leading scorer. He left for Southampton following relegation in 2003, having scored 130 goals in 235 appearances.

FACT 81

2000
THE
BLACK CATS

Sunderland formally adopted the nickname of the Black Cats in 2000, following the move to the Stadium of Light.

Black cats had been associated with the club for most of the twentieth century. The earliest known occasion was when Billy Hogg, a Sunderland player between 1899 and 1909, was photographed during that period with two teammates and a black cat.

A photograph taken around 1912 shows players with a black cat that used to be kept at Roker to catch rats. In 1937, a young fan smuggled a black kitten into Wembley for good luck at the FA Cup final. The first club crest also featured a black cat sitting on a football.

For as long as Sunderland fans could remember, they had been referring to their team as the Black Cats, with Rokerites much more of a term used by the press. A move from Roker Park meant the club looked at formalising a nickname, launching a poll with five options.

Black Cats was the overwhelming winner and it was formally adopted. For many the only surprise was that a poll was needed at all.

FACT 82
2003
WORST PREMIER LEAGUE SEASON EVER

Sunderland were relegated in 2002-03. A disastrous second half of the campaign saw them finish the season with just nineteen points, a new Premier League low.

After creditable seventh placed finishes in 2000 and 2001, the Black Cats only just avoided relegation in 2002, finishing seventeenth. They opened 2002-03 with one defeat from their first four games, but things went downhill very quickly.

After four defeats from five games, Peter Reid was sacked in October and replaced with Howard Wilkinson. As Christmas approached, Sunderland were very much in with a chance of survival. A 2-1 home win against Liverpool on 15th December lifted them out of the bottom three, but it turned out to be their last victory of the season.

It was clear that the problems lay in attack. Kevin Phillips finished top scorer for the sixth season running but this time he managed just six goals. Tore Andre Flo, a big money summer signing from Rangers, scored only four. In total, Sunderland scored just 21 goals all season.

On 18th January Sunderland lost 2-1 against Everton at Goodison Park. This was the first of fifteen successive defeats that left them cast adrift at the bottom. Wilkinson was sacked in March but replacement Mick McCarthy could not arrest the slide. They finished rock bottom with nineteen points, 25 from safety.

FACT 83

2004
PLAY-OFF PENALTY DEFEAT AGAIN

Sunderland failed to win promotion straight back to the Premier League in 2003-04. After a third placed finish, they lost a penalty shoot out to Crystal Palace in the play-off semi final.

After losing their opening two games, the Black Cats won seven out of ten to lift themselves into the play-off positions. Throughout the season they rarely looked like challenging for an automatic promotion spot.

Five successive wins in April brought hope of a late surge into the top two. However, the Black Cats lost a crucial home game against West Bromwich Albion which meant they were twelve points adrift with five games to go.

Sunderland lost 3-2 in the first leg of their semi-final at Selhurst Park, where all of the goals came in the second half. Back at the Stadium of Light, Kevin Kyle and Marcus Stewart scored late in the first half to give the Black Cats a 2-0 lead at the interval. However, despite going down to ten men, Palace scored a last gasp goal to take the tie into extra time.

There was no further scoring in the thirty added minutes and a shoot-out was needed. After five penalties each it was 4-4 but Jeff Whitley's sudden death kick was saved and Sunderland had lost in the cruellest fashion.

FACT 84
2004
MICHAEL GRAY LEAVES

Michael Gray, who has played more games than any other player for Sunderland in the Premier League era, left the club in 2004. The local boy had been with the club for twelve years and made 410 appearances.

Gray signed from school as an apprentice and got his first opportunities in the first team shortly after his eighteenth birthday in the 1992-93 season. He was a versatile player who could play anywhere down the left side of the field.

In 1995-96 Gray was an ever-present as Sunderland won promotion. He scored their first ever Premier League goal in a 4-1 win at Nottingham Forest in August 1996. The campaign ended in relegation and he then missed the decisive penalty in the shootout in the 1998 play-off final.

During 1998-99, when Sunderland were promoted back to the Premier League, Gray was again an ever-present. He was also capped three times by England but failed to make the squad for Euro 2000.

Gray's form dipped from 2001 and after Sunderland's relegation in 2003, he was stripped of the captaincy by manager Mick McCarthy. He spent the first half of 2003-04 on loan at Celtic then joined Blackburn Rovers for free when the January transfer window opened.

FACT 85
2005 CHAMPIONSHIP CHAMPIONS

Sunderland made no mistake in securing promotion in 2004-05. They finished top of the Championship, which had been rebranded from the First Division.

The Black Cats won just one of their first six, putting manager Mick McCarthy under pressure. However, the Board kept faith and September brought four straight wins to lift them up to fourth. Form dipped in early October, but after a 1-0 win over Millwall in their thirteenth game, they were never out of the play-off spots.

Over the Christmas period the Black Cats briefly climbed into the top two, but it was not until February that they seized control of the promotion race. A 4-1 win over Rotherham United on 22nd February was the first of eight successive victories that took them to the top of the table.

Reading ended the run by winning at the Stadium of Light on 9th April, but in their next game the Black Cats secured a crucial 2-2 draw at nearest challengers Ipswich.

On 23rd April Sunderland came from behind to beat Leicester City 2-1 in their penultimate home fixture. News that Ipswich could only draw at Leeds sparked jubilant scenes as promotion was secured. They then won 2-1 at West Ham United and beat Stoke City in front of a capacity home crowd to go up as champions.

FACT 86
2006
STRAIGHT BACK DOWN AS RECORD BREAKERS

Sunderland endured a horrendous season in 2005-06. They were relegated back to the Championship with just three wins from 38 games, breaking their own record for the lowest points in a Premier League season.

The Black Cats started the season with five straight defeats, before picking up their first point in a 1-1 home draw with West Bromwich Albion. There was then an encouraging 2-0 win at Middlesbrough followed by another 1-1 draw at the Stadium of Light, this time with West Ham United.

That mini revival had briefly lifted the Black Cats out of the bottom three going into the international break. When the Premier League resumed they lost 3-1 at home to Manchester United, the start of a nine game losing streak that finally came to an end on Boxing Day.

Mick McCarthy was sacked in March and Kevin Ball stepped up from the Academy on an interim basis, losing his first three games. Ironically it was one of the best results of the season, a 0-0 draw at Manchester United, that sealed the Black Cats' fate with five games remaining.

On 4th May Sunderland finally won at the Stadium of Light in the last home game of the season, beating Fulham 2-1. They finished on fifteen points, breaking their own unwanted record by four points.

FACT 87
2006
NIALL QUINN
TAKEOVER

In 2006 Sunderland saw a change of ownership when the Drumaville Consortium, led by former striker Niall Quinn, took control of the club.

Quinn played for Sunderland between 1996 and 2002, scoring 67 goals in 218 appearances. Although he was very much the figurehead of the takeover bid, he was one of nine businessmen involved with equal shares. The deal saw the club valued at £10 million and Drumaville took over 89% of the club shares.

Quinn became chairman and even appointed himself as manager as the Black Cats sought promotion back to the Premier League. After a poor start to his managerial career, he stepped aside and concentrated on boardroom duties.

In 2008 Drumaville sought new investors to fund the signing of new players. This led to Ellis Short buying a stake and the following year he put more money in to take full control.

Quinn did remain as club chairman however until 2011, when he was replaced by Short. After a brief spell as Director of International Development Quinn left the club in February 2012 to concentrate on family and business interests in Ireland. He was confident that the club was in the right hands and the BBC quoted him as saying "Everything is now in place for Sunderland to really make a statement, which was always my aim."

FACT 88
2007 CHAMPIONSHIP
CHAMPIONS AGAIN

Sunderland overcame a disastrous start to finish top of The Championship in 2006-07. A managerial change in August brought about an upturn in fortunes and a swift return to the Premier League.

Chairman Niall Quinn appointed himself as manager shortly before the start of the season. However, the campaign started with four straight defeats as well as a humiliating League Cup exit at Bury. Quinn stood aside and appointed former Manchester United captain Roy Keane in the week of August.

Keane won his first three games in charge but results were mixed in the autumn and at one point in November, the Black Cats were down in nineteenth place. Results did steadily improve and they were in the top half by the turn of the year.

On New Year's Day the Black Cats won 2-0 at Leicester City. This was the start of a seventeen-game unbeaten run that lifted them up to top spot with three games remaining. They then lost 3-1 at Colchester United but a 3-2 home win over Burnley meant promotion remained in their hands for the final game.

On 6th May Sunderland made no mistake, winning 5-0 at already relegated Luton Town. It meant they went up as champions, but it had been tight, just three points separating them from third place Derby County.

FACT 89
2007
RECORD FEE
FOR A GOALKEEPER

Sunderland made a clear statement of intent as they prepared for the 2007-08 Premier League campaign. They paid Scottish club Hearts £9 million for Craig Gordon, a British record for a goalkeeper.

Gordon was 24 years old and Scotland's first choice keeper. With Aston Villa also expressing an interest, the Black Cats had to make a record-breaking bid. In addition to being the highest price paid by a British club for a keeper, it was also a record fee for the Black Cats.

On his debut against Tottenham Hotspur at the Stadium of Light in the opening game of the season, Gordon kept a clean sheet in a 1-0 win. However, he briefly lost his place before Christmas when the Black Cats were thrashed 7-1 at Everton.

Gordon's time at Sunderland became marred by long spells on the side-lines due to knee injuries and also a broken arm sustained in a collision with his own player. Over five seasons he made 88 appearances, but still showed his quality with a stunning reflex save against Bolton in 2010. This was later voted the best save in twenty Premier League seasons.

After being released in 2012 Gordon was without a club for two years. He considered retirement but went on to reignite his career with Celtic, winning five Scottish titles.

FACT 90
2008 FIRST HOME DERBY WIN IN 28 YEARS

Sunderland finally won at home in the Tyne-Wear derby on 25th October 2008. Kieran Richardson's free kick fifteen minutes from time gave them a first home victory over Newcastle since 1980.

Djibril Cisse gave the Black Cats a twentieth minute lead, reacting well to turn in a wayward shot by Steed Malbranque. It was 1-1 at half time however thanks to a Shola Ameobi header.

The game was played in windy conditions, with Cisse and Ameobi both missing glorious opportunities to put their sides ahead in the second half. The Black Cats however were mastering the wind and got better as the game went on.

With fifteen minutes remaining El Hadji Diouf was felled on the edge of the penalty area. Richardson stepped up and hit an unstoppable free kick into the top corner that was measured at 73 miles per hour. Towards the end Cisse almost made it 3-1 but his shot came off the post and Sunderland held on for a deserved victory.

Afterwards Roy Keane said he had been reminded nine million times about the winless run, but that, "It's been a long time to wait but I think we deserved it. Mentally it was a big test today but we came through it with flying colours. We had to focus on the game, not past records."

FACT 91
2009
THE BEACH BALL GOAL

Sunderland scored one of the most bizarre goals of all time when they beat Liverpool 1-0 at the Stadium of Light on 17th October 2009. Keeper Pepe Reina looked set to save Darren Bent's shot until it was diverted into the net by a wayward beach ball.

The game was just five minutes old when Bent's shot went in off a beach ball that had been thrown onto the pitch by a visiting fan. Liverpool's players vehemently protested but the referee allowed the goal to stand.

Despite this good fortune, the Black Cats continued to show they were worthy of a victory. Bent also headed just wide and had an angled shot come back off the post. Liverpool almost snatched a draw in injury time but Craig Gordon made a superb double save from Dirk Kuyt and David N'Gog.

It was later accepted that the goal should not have stood. The rules of the game state that play should have been stopped until any foreign object was removed, then resumed with a drop ball. Referee Mike Jones was temporarily demoted to the Championship as a result.

Ten years on the BBC did a feature on the incident and Bent, who enjoyed a seventeen year career, recalled how this was the goal people spoke to him about the most.

FACT 92

2014 LEAGUE CUP FINALISTS

Sunderland played at the new Wembley for the first time in 2014. They reached the League Cup final following a memorable penalty shoot-out victory over Manchester United, but their hopes of glory were quashed when they were then beaten 3-1 by Manchester City.

In the semi-final the Black Cats were paired with Manchester United and won the first game 2-1 at the Stadium of Light. The second leg went into extra time as United led 1-0 after ninety minutes.

With an away goals defeat looming, Phil Bardsley's shot was pushed into the net by United keeper David de Gea, sending 9,000 travelling fans delirious. United scored a last gasp winner to force a penalty shoot-out, but Vito Mannone saved twice to take the Black Cats to the new Wembley for the first time since it opened in 2007.

Ten minutes into the final Sunderland took the lead through Fabio Borini. Later in the first half he had a great chance to score again but Vincent Kompany made a last gasp challenge.

Sunderland were still ahead at half time but City struck back to score twice in a minute before the hour mark. As the Black Cats pressed for an equaliser, they conceded again in injury time to leave them still seeking a first trophy since 1973.

FACT 93
2015
A DOUBLE DERBY DOUBLE

Sunderland well and truly secured Tyne-Wear derby bragging rights in 2014-15. For the second season running, they won both Premier League games against their great rivals.

The first of these derbies was at the Stadium of Light in October 2014. Steven Fletcher scored early for the Black Cats but after 57 minutes Newcastle were level. With six minutes remaining, Fabio Borini got the winning goal.

Later in the season Borini was on target again at St James Park. He scored the opening goal from the penalty spot as Sunderland cruised to a 3-0 victory.

The first derby of 2014-15 was at St James Park the weekend before Christmas. Adam Johnson's last-minute winner was scored on the counter attack, giving the Black Cats only their third league win of the season.

At the Stadium of Light on 5th April, Jermaine Defoe scored the only goal of the game with a stunning volley on the stroke of half time. The Black Cats had now won five games in succession against Newcastle.

Sunderland made it six in a row with a 3-0 victory at the Stadium of Light the following October. The run finally came to an end on 20th March 2016 when the two sides drew 1-1 at St James Park.

FACT 94
2016 CLUB TRANSFER RECORD

Sunderland broke their transfer record in 2016 when they paid £13.6 million for Dider Ndong. Despite an impressive first season with the Black Cats, his relationship soured after a second successive relegation in 2018 and he was eventually sacked for breach of contract.

Gabon international midfielder Ndong joined the Black Cats from French side Lorient at the end of the August transfer window. He made his debut as a substitute in a 3-0 home defeat to Everton on 12th September but became a key member of the side that season, starting 27 times in the league.

Ndong's only goal for the Black Cats was a superb curling effort in a 4-0 win at Crystal Palace in February 2017. Although they were relegated, he remained and was a regular in the first half of 2017-18. He moved to Premier League Watford on loan in January but made the bench just three times and did not get on the pitch.

After relegation to League One, Ndong failed to reappear for pre-season training and angered fans by posting a picture on Instagram of himself by a hotel pool. When he finally returned at the end of September, he was served with a dismissal notice for breach of contract and signed for French side En Avant Guingamp later in the year.

FACT 95

2017
RELEGATED

After ten years in the Premier League, Sunderland were relegated in 2016-17. They finished bottom of the table with just 24 points, sixteen adrift of safety.

In the close season Sam Allardyce left to take the England job. He was replaced by David Moyes, who told fans to expect the season to be a battle for survival. The Black Cats had a disastrous start, losing eight of their first ten games.

A brief rally in November saw the Black Cats win three from four. This lifted them to third from bottom, but they were never out of the relegation zone all season. The attack was clearly the problem, with the Black Cats failing to score in twenty of their 38 games. They scored just 29 all season, with leading scorer Jermaine Defoe netting fifteen of them.

On 21st January Sunderland lost 2-0 at West Bromwich Albion to fall back to the bottom, where they remained for the rest of the campaign. Their fate was sealed on 29th April when Bournemouth won 1-0 at the Stadium of Light, condemning Sunderland to the Championship with four games still remaining.

FACT 96

2018
DOWN AGAIN

Sunderland endured a disastrous season in 2017-18 when they were relegated to League One. They had three managers and finished rock bottom of the Championship to drop to the third tier for only the second time in the club's history.

After the dismissal of David Moyes, Simon Grayson replaced him as manager. However just one win in the opening fifteen league games saw him sacked at the end of October. First team coach Robbie Stockdale took over on a caretaker basis, failing to win any of his three games in temporary charge before Chris Coleman was appointed in late November.

Coleman oversaw a mini revival of one defeat in five games that lifted the Black Cats out of the relegation one at the turn of the year. However, they then won just three of their last twenty games. Relegation was confirmed with two games remaining, when Sunderland lost 2-1 at home to fellow strugglers Burton Albion on 21st April.

Coleman was then sacked before the end of the season, with Stockdale taking temporary charge for a 3-0 victory over Wolverhampton Wanderers. It was only the third home win of the season, but there was some optimism by the presence in the stands of Stewart Donald, who was close to a deal to take control of the club.

FACT 97

2019 PLAY-OFF FINALISTS

Sunderland failed to bounce straight back up to the Championship in 2018-19. A late season slump in form meant they had to settle for the play-offs, where they were beaten by a last-gasp Charlton Athletic goal in the final.

Former St Mirren boss Jack Ross was appointed as manager and Sunderland started well, losing just twice before Christmas. On Boxing Day the Black Cats beat Bradford at the Stadium of Light, the first of nineteen games unbeaten. This meant with six games remaining promotion was in their own hands.

A crazy game on 19th April saw Sunderland lose 5-4 at home to Coventry City. They recovered to beat Doncaster Rovers 2-0 but then could only draw 1-1 at Peterborough United and against fellow hopefuls Portsmouth at home. This meant automatic promotion was out of their hands and they lost their last two games, at Fleetwood Town and Southend United but were sure of a play-off place.

In the semi-final Sunderland beat Portsmouth 1-0 at home then drew 0-0 at Fratton Park. In the final against Charlton the game looked set for extra time with the sides level at 1-1. Then deep into injury time Patrick Bauer scored to inflict what Ross described as a 'gut-wrenching defeat' on the Black Cats.

FACT 98
2020 CURTAILED SEASON

Sunderland's second attempt at getting out of League One was curtailed by the Covid 19 pandemic. When clubs voted to use a points per game basis to determine the final table, Sunderland just missed out on the play-offs.

Manager Jack Ross was sacked after winning just five of the opening ten games. He was replaced by Phil Parkinson and although his early results were mixed, an upturn of form after Christmas saw the Black Cats move into the play-off places.

Along with all other English league fixtures, Sunderland's home game with Blackpool on 14th March was called off as Covid-19 hospitalisations surged. On 3rd April the Football League was curtailed indefinitely until it was safe to resume playing. Although the Premier League and Championship did restart, League One and Two clubs voted not to play on and use points per game to determine positions.

Sunderland's poor form immediately prior to the curtailment went against them. The table was very tight and they were only a point off the play-off positions with ten games to go, but had also played a game more than most of their rivals. When points were calculated, Sunderland dropped a further place to eighth in the final table, their worst ever final position.

FACT 99
2021 EFL TROPHY WINNERS

After seven successive Wembley defeats, Sunderland finally lifted a trophy there in 2021. However, their EFL Trophy success was played behind closed doors due to the ongoing Covid-19 pandemic.

The Black Cats finished second in the group containing Aston Villa Under 21's, Carlisle United and Fleetwood Town. They then won 2-1 at Oldham Athletic, 2-0 against Port Vale 2-0 at home in the last sixteen and 3-0 at Milton Keynes Dons in the quarter final. In the semi-final at the Stadium of Light, they beat Lincoln City 5-3 on penalties after a 1-1 draw.

Sunderland's opponents at Wembley were Tranmere Rovers. Covid-19 meant there were no fans present as they sought to end a dreadful run of defeats in finals there — one FA Cup, two League Cup, one EFL Trophy and three play-offs.

The game was not a classic and Lee Burge made some important saves. In the 57th minute Aiden McGeady's perfect through pass found Lynden Gooch, who kept his cool to slot the ball past the keeper.

Sunderland held on for victory to the relief of their fans watching at home in Wearside. The club had finally won a trophy after 48 years. It was just four weeks after Kyril Louis-Dreyfus had taken control of the club, hopefully marking the start of a new era.

FACT 100
2021
BEATEN IN THE PLAY-OFFS AGAIN

Although the Covid-19 pandemic continued, the League One 2020-21 season was played to a finish. Sunderland again lost out in the play-offs, being beaten in the semi-final by Lincoln City.

Covid restrictions meant all of Sunderland's 46 league games were played behind closed doors. Phil Parkinson was sacked after thirteen games with the Black Cats outside the play-off places. Lee Johnson took charge and a run of nine wins from twelve took them within two points of an automatic promotion spot with eight matches to play.

Sunderland then won just once more to finish in fourth, ten points behind second placed Peterborough United. An easing of restrictions meant the play-offs were played in front of a limited number of spectators. The first game at Sincil Bank saw the Black Cats lose 2-0, with both Lincoln goals coming in the second half.

The return game at the Stadium of Light took place before a crowd of 10,000. Aiden McGeady set up both Ross Stewart and Charlie Wyke to level the tie before half time, but Lincoln's Tom Hopper headed them back into the ascendancy in the 56th minute.

Despite their best efforts, which included McGeady hitting the post, Sunderland couldn't overcome the deficit and were left facing a fourth season in the third tier.

The 100 Facts Series

Arsenal, *Steve Horton*	978-1-908724-09-0
Aston Villa, *Steve Horton*	978-1-908724-98-4
Brighton, *Steve Horton*	978-1-912782-78-9
Celtic, *Steve Horton*	978-1-908724-10-6
Chelsea, *Kristian Downer*	978-1-908724-11-3
Everton, *Bob Sharp*	978-1-908724-12-0
Hearts, *Steve Horton*	978-1-912782-48-2
Leeds, *Steve Horton*	978-1-908724-94-6
Leicester City, *Steve Horton*	978-1-912782-47-5
Liverpool, *Steve Horton*	978-1-908724-13-7
Manchester City, *Steve Horton*	978-1-908724-14-4
Manchester United, *Iain McCartney*	978-1-908724-15-1
Newcastle United, *Steve Horton*	978-1-908724-16-8
Norwich City, *Steve Horton*	978-1-908724-99-1
Nottingham Forest, *Steve Horton*	978-1-912782-46-8
Rangers, *David Clayton*	978-1-908724-17-5
Sheffield United, *Steve Horton*	978-1-912782-45-1
Southampton, *Steve Horton*	978-1-912782-79-6
Sunderland, *Steve Horton*	978-1-912782-80-2
Tottenham Hotspur, *Steve Horton*	978-1-908724-18-2
West Ham, *Steve Horton*	978-1-908724-80-9

Player Autographs

Player Autographs

Player Autographs